IELTS

GENERAL TRAINING 18

WITH ANSWERS

AUTHENTIC PRACTICE TESTS

Shaftesbury Road, Cambridge CB2 8EA, United Kingdom

One Liberty Plaza, 20th Floor, New York, NY 10006, USA

477 Williamstown Road, Port Melbourne, VIC 3207, Australia

314–321, 3rd Floor, Plot 3, Splendor Forum, Jasola District Centre, New Delhi – 110025, India

103 Penang Road, #05–06/07, Visioncrest Commercial, Singapore 238467

Cambridge University Press & Assessment is a department of the University of Cambridge.

We share the University's mission to contribute to society through the pursuit of education, learning and research at the highest international levels of excellence.

www.cambridge.org
Information on this title: www.cambridge.org/9781009275194

First published 2023
20 19 18 17 16 15 14 13 12 11 10 9 8 7 6 5 4

Printed in Malaysia by Vivar Printing

A catalogue record for this publication is available from the British Library

ISBN 978-1-009-27519-4 General Training Student's Book with Answers with Audio with Resource Bank

Contents

Introduction

Prepare for the exam with practice tests from Cambridge

Inside you'll find four authentic examination papers from Cambridge University Press & Assessment. They are the perfect way to practise – EXACTLY like the real exam.

Why are they unique?

All our authentic practice tests go through the same design process as the IELTS test. We check every single part of our practice tests with real students under exam conditions, to make sure we give you the most authentic experience possible.

Students can take these tests on their own or with the help of a teacher to familiarise themselves with the exam format, understand the scoring system and practise exam technique.

Further information

IELTS is jointly managed by the British Council, IDP: IELTS Australia and Cambridge University Press & Assessment. Further information can be found on the IELTS official website at ielts.org.

WHAT IS THE TEST FORMAT?

IELTS consists of four components. All candidates take the same Listening and Speaking tests. There is a choice of Reading and Writing tests according to whether a candidate is taking the Academic or General Training module.

Academic	General Training
For candidates wishing to study at undergraduate or postgraduate levels, and for those seeking professional registration.	For candidates wishing to migrate to an English-speaking country (Australia, Canada, New Zealand, UK), and for those wishing to train or study below degree level.

The test components are taken in the following order:

Listening 4 parts, 40 items, approximately 30 minutes		
Academic Reading 3 sections, 40 items 60 minutes	or	**General Training Reading** 3 sections, 40 items 60 minutes
Academic Writing 2 tasks 60 minutes	or	**General Training Writing** 2 tasks 60 minutes
Speaking 11 to 14 minutes		
Total (Maximum) Test Time 2 hours 44 minutes		

GENERAL TRAINING TEST FORMAT

Listening

This test consists of four parts, each with ten questions. The first two parts are concerned with social needs. The first part is a conversation between two speakers and the second part is a monologue. The final two parts are concerned with situations related to educational or training contexts. The third part is a conversation between up to four people and the fourth part is a monologue.

A variety of question types is used, including: multiple choice, matching, plan/map/diagram labelling, form completion, note completion, table completion, flowchart completion, summary completion, sentence completion and short-answer questions.

Candidates hear the recording once only and answer the questions as they listen. Ten minutes are allowed at the end for candidates to transfer their answers to the answer sheet.

Reading

This test consists of 3 sections with 40 questions. The texts are taken from notices, advertisements, leaflets, newspapers, instruction manuals, books and magazines. The first section contains texts relevant to basic linguistic survival in English, with tasks mainly concerned with providing factual information. The second section focuses on the work context and involves texts containing more complex language. The third section involves reading more extended texts, with a more complex structure, but with the emphasis on descriptive and instructive rather than argumentative texts.

A variety of question types is used, including: multiple choice, identifying information (True/False/Not Given), identifying the writer's views/claims (Yes/No/Not Given), matching information, matching headings, matching features, matching sentence endings, sentence completion, summary completion, note completion, table completion, flowchart completion, diagram-label completion and short-answer questions.

Writing

This test consists of two tasks. It is suggested that candidates spend about 20 minutes on Task 1, which requires them to write at least 150 words, and 40 minutes on Task 2, which requires them to write at least 250 words. Task 2 contributes twice as much as Task 1 to the Writing score.

In Task 1, candidates are asked to respond to a given situation with a letter requesting information or explaining the situation. They are assessed on their ability to engage in personal correspondence, elicit and provide general factual information, express needs, wants, likes and dislikes, express opinions, complaints, etc.

In Task 2, candidates are presented with a point of view, argument or problem. They are assessed on their ability to provide general factual information, outline a problem and present a solution, present and justify an opinion, and evaluate and challenge ideas, evidence or arguments.

Candidates are also assessed on their ability to write in an appropriate style. More information on assessing the Writing test, including Writing assessment criteria (public version), is available at ielts.org.

Speaking

This test takes between 11 and 14 minutes and is conducted by a trained examiner. There are three parts:

Part 1

The candidate and the examiner introduce themselves. Candidates then answer general questions about themselves, their home/family, their job/studies, their interests and a wide range of similar familiar topic areas. This part lasts between four and five minutes.

Part 2

The candidate is given a task card with prompts and is asked to talk on a particular topic. The candidate has one minute to prepare and they can make some notes if they wish, before speaking for between one and two minutes. The examiner then asks one or two questions on the same topic.

Part 3

The examiner and the candidate engage in a discussion of more abstract issues which are thematically linked to the topic in Part 2. The discussion lasts between four and five minutes.

The Speaking test assesses whether candidates can communicate effectively in English. The assessment takes into account Fluency and Coherence, Lexical Resource, Grammatical Range and Accuracy, and Pronunciation. More information on assessing the Speaking test, including Speaking assessment criteria (public version), is available at ielts.org.

HOW IS IELTS SCORED?

IELTS results are reported on a nine-band scale. In addition to the score for overall language ability, IELTS provides a score in the form of a profile for each of the four skills (Listening, Reading, Writing and Speaking). These scores are also reported on a nine-band scale. All scores are recorded on the Test Report Form along with details of the candidate's nationality, first language and date of birth. Each Overall Band Score corresponds to a descriptive statement which gives a summary of the English-language ability of a candidate classified at that level. The nine bands and their descriptive statements are as follows:

9 ***Expert user*** *– Has fully operational command of the language: appropriate, accurate and fluent with complete understanding.*

8 ***Very good user*** *– Has fully operational command of the language with only occasional unsystematic inaccuracies and inappropriacies. Misunderstandings may occur in unfamiliar situations. Handles complex detailed argumentation well.*

7 ***Good user*** *– Has operational command of the language, though with occasional inaccuracies, inappropriacies and misunderstandings in some situations. Generally handles complex language well and understands detailed reasoning.*

6 ***Competent user*** *– Has generally effective command of the language despite some inaccuracies, inappropriacies and misunderstandings. Can use and understand fairly complex language, particularly in familiar situations.*

5 ***Modest user*** *– Has partial command of the language, coping with overall meaning in most situations, though is likely to make many mistakes. Should be able to handle basic communication in own field.*

4 ***Limited user*** *– Basic competence is limited to familiar situations. Has frequent problems in understanding and expression. Is not able to use complex language.*

3 ***Extremely limited user*** *– Conveys and understands only general meaning in very familiar situations. Frequent breakdowns in communication occur.*

2 ***Intermittent user*** *– Has great difficulty understanding spoken and written English.*

1 ***Non-user*** *– Essentially has no ability to use the language beyond possibly a few isolated words.*

0 ***Did not attempt the test*** *– Did not answer the questions.*

MARKING THE PRACTICE TESTS

Listening and Reading

The answer keys are on pages 123–130.
Each question in the Listening and Reading tests is worth one mark.

Questions which require letter / Roman numeral answers

For questions where the answers are letters or Roman numerals, you should write *only* the number of answers required. For example, if the answer is a single letter or numeral, you should write only one answer. If you have written more letters or numerals than are required, the answer must be marked wrong.

Questions which require answers in the form of words or numbers

- Answers may be written in upper or lower case.
- Words in brackets are *optional* – they are correct, but not necessary.
- Alternative answers are separated by a slash (/).
- If you are asked to write an answer using a certain number of words and/or (a) number(s), you will be penalised if you exceed this. For example, if a question specifies an answer using NO MORE THAN THREE WORDS and the correct answer is 'black leather coat', the answer 'coat of black leather' is *incorrect*.
- In questions where you are expected to complete a gap, you should only transfer the necessary missing word(s) onto the answer sheet. For example, to complete 'in the …', where the correct answer is 'morning', the answer 'in the morning' would be *incorrect*.
- All answers require correct spelling (including words in brackets).
- Both US and UK spelling are acceptable and are included in the answer key.
- All standard alternatives for numbers, dates and currencies are acceptable.
- All standard abbreviations are acceptable.
- You will find additional notes about individual answers in the answer key.

Writing

The sample answers are on pages 131–139. It is not possible for you to give yourself a mark for the Writing tasks. We have provided high-level model answers written by examiners, with commentaries. Additional sample and model answers can be downloaded from the Resource Bank. These sample and model answers will give you an insight into what is required for the Writing test.

HOW SHOULD YOU INTERPRET YOUR SCORES?

At the end of each Listening and Reading answer key you will find a chart which will help you assess whether, on the basis of your practice test results, you are ready to take the IELTS test.

In interpreting your score, there are a number of points you should bear in mind. Your performance in the real IELTS test will be reported in two ways: there will be a Band Score from 1 to 9 for each of the components and an Overall Band Score from 1 to 9, which is the average of your scores in the four components. However, institutions considering your application are advised to look at both the Overall Band Score and the Band Score for each component in order to determine whether you have the language skills needed for a particular course of study or work environment. For example, if you are applying for a course which involves a lot of reading and writing, but no lectures, listening skills might be less important and a score of 5 in Listening might be acceptable if the Overall Band Score was 7. However, for a course which has lots of lectures and spoken instructions, a score of 5 in Listening might be unacceptable even though the Overall Band Score was 7.

Once you have marked your tests, you should have some idea of whether your listening and reading skills are good enough for you to try the IELTS test. If you did well enough in one component, but not in others, you will have to decide for yourself whether you are ready to take the test.

The practice tests have been checked to ensure that they are the same level of difficulty as the real IELTS test. However, we cannot guarantee that your score in the practice tests will be reflected in the real IELTS test. The practice tests can only give you an idea of your possible future performance and it is ultimately up to you to make decisions based on your score.

Different institutions accept different IELTS scores for different types of courses. We have based our recommendations on the average scores which the majority of institutions accept. The institution to which you are applying may, of course, require a higher or lower score than most other institutions.

Test 1

LISTENING

Listening test audio

PART 1 *Questions 1–10*

Complete the notes below.

Write ***ONE WORD AND/OR A NUMBER*** *for each answer.*

Transport survey

Name:	Sadie Jones
Year of birth:	1991
Postcode:	**1** ....

Travelling by bus

Date of bus journey:	**2** ....
Reason for trip:	shopping and visit to the **3** ....
Travelled by bus because cost of	**4** .... too high
Got on bus at	**5** .... Street
Complaints about bus service:	- bus today was **6** ....
	- frequency of buses in the **7** ....

Travelling by car

Goes to the	**8** .... by car

Travelling by bicycle

Dislikes travelling by bike in the city centre because of the **9** ....

Doesn't own a bike because of a lack of **10** ....

→ p. 123 p. 103

PART 2 *Questions 11–20*

Questions 11–13

*Choose the correct letter, **A**, **B** or **C**.*

Becoming a volunteer for ACE

11 Why does the speaker apologise about the seats?

A They are too small.
B There are not enough of them.
C Some of them are very close together.

12 What does the speaker say about the age of volunteers?

A The age of volunteers is less important than other factors.
B Young volunteers are less reliable than older ones.
C Most volunteers are about 60 years old.

13 What does the speaker say about training?

A It is continuous.
B It is conducted by a manager.
C It takes place online.

Questions 14 and 15

*Choose **TWO** letters, **A–E**.*

Which **TWO** issues does the speaker ask the audience to consider before they apply to be volunteers?

A their financial situation
B their level of commitment
C their work experience
D their ambition
E their availability

Questions 16–20

What does the speaker suggest would be helpful for each of the following areas of voluntary work?

*Choose **FIVE** answers from the box and write the correct letter, **A–G**, next to Questions 16–20.*

Helpful things volunteers might offer

A experience on stage
B original, new ideas
C parenting skills
D an understanding of food and diet
E retail experience
F a good memory
G a good level of fitness

Area of voluntary work

16 Fundraising ....
17 Litter collection ....
18 'Playmates' ....
19 Story club ....
20 First aid ....

 ➔ p. 123 p. 104

PART 3 *Questions 21–30*

Questions 21–26

Choose the correct letter, ***A****,* ***B*** *or* ***C****.*

Talk on jobs in fashion design

21 What problem did Chantal have at the start of the talk?

- **A** Her view of the speaker was blocked.
- **B** She was unable to find an empty seat.
- **C** The students next to her were talking.

22 What were Hugo and Chantal surprised to hear about the job market?

- **A** It has become more competitive than it used to be.
- **B** There is more variety in it than they had realised.
- **C** Some areas of it are more exciting than others.

23 Hugo and Chantal agree that the speaker's message was

- **A** unfair to them at times.
- **B** hard for them to follow.
- **C** critical of the industry.

24 What do Hugo and Chantal criticise about their school careers advice?

- **A** when they received the advice
- **B** how much advice was given
- **C** who gave the advice

25 When discussing their future, Hugo and Chantal disagree on

- **A** which is the best career in fashion.
- **B** when to choose a career in fashion.
- **C** why they would like a career in fashion.

26 How does Hugo feel about being an unpaid assistant?

- **A** He is realistic about the practice.
- **B** He feels the practice is dishonest.
- **C** He thinks others want to change the practice.

Questions 27 and 28

*Choose **TWO** letters, **A–E**.*

Which **TWO** mistakes did the speaker admit she made in her first job?

A being dishonest to her employer
B paying too much attention to how she looked
C expecting to become well known
D trying to earn a lot of money
E openly disliking her client

Questions 29 and 30

*Choose **TWO** letters, **A–E**.*

Which **TWO** pieces of retail information do Hugo and Chantal agree would be useful?

A the reasons people return fashion items
B how much time people have to shop for clothes
C fashion designs people want but can't find
D the best time of year for fashion buying
E the most popular fashion sizes

 → p. 123 p. 105

PART 4 *Questions 31–40*

Complete the notes below.

Write ***ONE WORD ONLY*** *for each answer.*

Elephant translocation

Reasons for overpopulation at Majete National Park

- strict enforcement of anti-poaching laws
- successful breeding

Problems caused by elephant overpopulation

- greater competition, causing hunger for elephants
- damage to **31** .... in the park

The translocation process

- a suitable group of elephants from the same **32** .... was selected
- vets and park staff made use of **33** .... to help guide the elephants into an open plain
- elephants were immobilised with tranquilisers
  - this process had to be completed quickly to reduce **34** ....
  - elephants had to be turned on their **35** .... to avoid damage to their lungs
  - elephants' **36** .... had to be monitored constantly
  - tracking devices were fitted to the matriarchs
  - data including the size of their tusks and **37** .... was taken
- elephants were taken by truck to their new reserve

Advantages of translocation at Nkhotakota Wildlife Park

- **38** .... opportunities
- a reduction in the number of poachers and **39** ....
- an example of conservation that other parks can follow
- an increase in **40** .... as a contributor to GDP

READING

SECTION 1 *Questions 1–14*

Read the text below and answer Questions 1–7.

What to do if your clothes have been lost or damaged by a dry cleaner

Dry cleaners are legally required to take reasonable care of anything left with them. You can claim compensation if your belongings are damaged or lost while in their care.

Even if the dry cleaning company has a sign saying they aren't responsible for items left with them, this isn't necessarily true. They can't opt out of this responsibility just by putting up a sign.

As soon as you realise there's a problem, contact them and explain the situation. They might offer you compensation straight away. If they don't, you should ask them to either cover the cost of repairing the item or to pay for a replacement (if it can't be repaired).

If they have to pay the cost of replacing a damaged or lost item, the maximum they're obliged to offer you is the value of the item when it was left with them, not what it would cost to replace as new. You'll probably be asked to provide evidence of how much it originally cost – for example, a receipt. The dry cleaner can then offer you a reduced amount depending on the condition of the item – you'll have to negotiate the cost with them.

If the dry cleaner is part of a national chain, you could get in touch with the customer services department of their head office and make the complaint to them directly.

If the dry cleaner refuses to compensate you or they offer you too little, try the following steps:

- If the dry cleaner is a member of a trade association such as the UK Fashion and Textile Association, you can pass your complaint to them and they may be able to help you.

- You could get an independent organisation to look at your issue and produce a report, but this could be expensive (often around £100).

If you've tried the options above and are still unhappy with the outcome, you could take your case to court. There's a time limit for going to court – from when you took the item to the dry cleaner, you have up to six years.

Questions 1–7

Do the following statements agree with the information given in the text on page 16?

In boxes 1–7 on your answer sheet, write

TRUE	*if the statement agrees with the information*
FALSE	*if the statement contradicts the information*
NOT GIVEN	*if there is no information on this*

1 Dry cleaners are generally responsible for items left with them, even if there's a sign saying the opposite.

2 If the dry cleaner loses an item belonging to you, they should give you enough money to buy a completely new one.

3 If you have the receipt for a damaged item, the company should refund the amount you originally paid for it.

4 It may be possible to get support for your complaint from a dry cleaners' trade association.

5 If you're offered too little compensation, you can request a free report from an independent organisation.

6 Most people who take a case about a dry-cleaning company to court are satisfied with the outcome.

7 If an item was lost or damaged nine months ago, you can still take the dry cleaner to court.

Read the text below and answer Questions 8–14.

Groups for readers and writers

A Teenvision

This is a reading group for teens aged 12–16 which meets on the last Thursday of the month. We are a friendly group, with everybody keen to talk about what we've enjoyed reading recently and make suggestions on what we should read next. We are massive fans of action, fantasy and adventure but we try to include a mix of genres in our choices.

B Creative writing workshops

Would you like to share your writing with others and hear their constructive suggestions for how to improve it? Have you got a book inside you but need the inspiration to get started? Build your confidence to begin formulating ideas for storylines and characters at our regular workshops. Open to all – beginners and established writers.

C Books for now

We meet on the second and fourth Mondays of each month in members' homes. The group is open to men and women who enjoy discussing the themes and issues found in science fiction novels. Our books are usually those written from the 1960s onwards and include feminist science fiction, cyberpunk and scientific romance.

D Readers' book group

This is an open group for parents at the library, and toddlers are welcome to come along and play in the children's library while the meeting is taking place. The group reads mainly fiction of different genres. Books are supplied by the library. Anyone is welcome – have a look at our website to see what the book is for the next meeting.

E The book club

Every month members of this group read a fabulous business book which is then discussed when we meet. At our meetings you'll have the chance to network with other members – all like-minded businesswomen – in a relaxed environment. There will be lots of ideas to discuss, as well as refreshments and lots of fun!

F Poetry writing group

A writing group for young poets aged between 12 and 18 at the library. You will explore how to power up your imagination, and your poems will be displayed in the library and online. The group meets fortnightly on Saturdays from 12 p.m. to 2 p.m. The group is currently full but anyone interested is welcome to join the membership waiting list.

Questions 8–14

The text on page 18 has six paragraphs, **A–F**.

Which paragraph mentions the following?

*Write the correct letter, **A–F**, in boxes 8–14 on your answer sheet.*

NB *You may use any letter more than once.*

8 Members of this group share ideas for the books they would like to read.

9 It isn't possible for any new members to join this group at present.

10 You can get feedback on your own work from other members of this group.

11 This group focuses on stories belonging to just one genre.

12 Work produced by members of this group will be available to the public.

13 This group doesn't read or write either poetry or fiction.

14 This group would suit someone who thinks they could write a book.

→ p. 124

SECTION 2 *Questions 15–27*

Read the text below and answer Questions 15–22.

Mechanical lifting equipment

If some simple precautions are taken, lifting equipment that is essential for construction and engineering projects can be used safely. Forklift trucks, lifting trolleys, mobile and fixed cranes and all their parts are classed as lifting equipment.

All equipment used for lifting or moving heavy loads should be properly constructed. For example, equipment bearing a CE mark has been constructed to international standards. In addition, equipment that meets these standards will have documented instructions for tests that should be adhered to prior to using the equipment. Certain types of machinery, such as cranes, must be inspected by a qualified engineer on a six-monthly basis.

For operations that use cranes, a formal lift plan must be prepared. Lift plans are a type of risk assessment, whereby the possible dangers of the operation are carefully calculated, and control measures are identified and put in place. Before any lift proceeds, the plan should be talked over with the lifting crew during what is often referred to as a 'Tool Box Talk' (TBT). This is an important opportunity for them to ask questions about their role in the operation.

When heavy loads are being moved around, there are some practical things that should be done to prevent accidents. Firstly, if a load needs to be moved where workers or members of the public are present, the area must have barriers or other means to ensure no one is allowed to walk under the load while it is moving. Secondly, someone called a banksman should always be used when moving heavy loads by crane. As a crane driver often cannot see the load, especially during touch-down, this person tells him or her which way to move it.

It is very unusual for machinery such as cranes to fail. However, it is all too easy to ignore the importance of the secondary equipment. This refers to those items that are attached between the mechanical lifting machine and the load that is being lifted. Chains, slings, shackles and rigging are all examples of secondary lifting equipment, and it is perhaps surprising to note that most injuries occur due to faults or weaknesses in these items. It is essential that a six-monthly visual inspection is carried out to ensure there are no signs of wear or damage to the slings and shackles.

Questions 15–22

Complete the notes below.

Choose **NO MORE THAN TWO WORDS** *from the text for each answer.*

Write your answers in boxes 15–22 on your answer sheet.

Lifting equipment

- must be manufactured well, e.g., have a **15** .... on it
- may need to undergo **16** .... before use
- may need a regular check by an **17** ....

Lift plans

- relevant to cranes
- used to establish and carry out **18** .... for any risks
- a **19** .... can be consulted during a 'Tool Box Talk'

Preventing accidents with heavy loads

- use objects such as **20** .... to make sure the load doesn't pass over anyone's head
- appoint a **21** .... to give verbal directions to the crane driver

Secondary lifting equipment (chains, slings, etc.)

- more likely to cause **22** ....

Read the text below and answer Questions 23–27.

Dealing with customer complaints

When a customer complains, it is usually for a good reason. Here are some strategies that will help you handle a customer complaint in a smooth and professional manner.

When a customer presents you with a complaint, keep in mind that the issue is not personal. Aiming to win the confrontation accomplishes nothing. He or she has usually made a purchase that did not meet their expectations – a product, service, or maybe a combination of the two. A worker who remains in control of their emotions deals from a position of strength.

Let the customer say what they need to. Respond with phrases such as, 'Hmm', 'I see', and 'Tell me more'. Then be quiet. As the customer expresses their annoyance yet sees you are not reacting, he or she will begin to relax. The customer needs to do this before being able to hear your solution.

When the customer has calmed down and feels you have heard his or her side, start asking questions. Be careful not to give scripted replies but use this as an opportunity to start a genuine conversation, building a relationship of trust with your customer. To help you understand the situation, get as many details as possible.

Take charge of the situation and let the customer know what you are going to do to solve the problem. One thing to keep in mind is that you should know what you can and cannot do within the policy of the business you work for. The cost could be minimal – maybe a simple upgrade on the customer's next purchase or a small gift certificate. A simple gesture like this could result in a word-of-mouth recommendation to others, while making a promise you cannot commit to will only set you back.

Questions 23–27

Complete the table below.

Choose **ONE WORD ONLY** *from the text for each answer.*

Write your answers in boxes 23–27 on your answer sheet.

Strategies for dealing with customer complaints		
Strategy	**Your approach**	**The customer …**
Stay calm	• Remember it is not a direct attack on you. • Do not try to **23** ………………… the argument.	• usually had **24** ………………… that were not fulfilled.
Listen well	• Use short phrases in reply.	• cannot recognise a **25** ………………… until calm.
Get the facts	• Ask questions and begin a proper conversation.	• will start to trust you.
Suggest action	• Be sure of your company's **26** ………………… on complaints.	• may well make a verbal **27** ………………… in future.

→ p. 124

SECTION 3 *Questions 28–40*

Read the text on pages 25 and 26 and answer Questions 28–40.

Questions 28–33

The text on pages 25 and 26 has six sections, **A–F**.

Choose the correct heading for each section from the list of headings below.

*Write the correct number, **i–viii**, in boxes 28–33 on your answer sheet.*

List of Headings

- **i** An enterprise arising from success in other countries
- **ii** The hope that storks will inspire a range of emotions and actions
- **iii** Support from some organisations but not from others
- **iv** Finding new types of habitat
- **v** Opposition from the general public
- **vi** A sign of hope in difficult times
- **vii** Creatures which represent both joy and opposition
- **viii** Storks causing delight and the revival of public events

28 Section **A**

29 Section **B**

30 Section **C**

31 Section **D**

32 Section **E**

33 Section **F**

White storks back in Britain after hundreds of years

These beautiful birds could be about to become a feature of the British landscape again

A The last definitive record of a pair of white storks successfully breeding in Britain was in 1416, from a nest on St Giles Cathedral in Edinburgh. No one knows why storks disappeared from our shores. They often featured on the menus of medieval banquets so we might, quite simply, have consumed them all. But there could be a more ominous reason. Storks are migrants arriving after the end of winter, nesting on rooftops and happily associating with humans, and because of this they have long been a symbol of hope and new life. Yet their association with rebirth also meant they became a symbol of rebellion. Shortly after the restoration of King Charles II in 1660, while storks were rare but surviving, parliament debated putting greater effort into destroying them entirely for fear they might inspire republicanism. Today, fortunately, that notion has disappeared and the stork retains its association with new life, appearing on cards given to celebrate the arrival of a new child, as a bird carrying a baby in a sling held in its beak.

B So, after such a long absence, there was great excitement when in April of this year a pair of white storks built an untidy nest of sticks in the top branches of a huge oak in the middle of our rewilding project at Knepp Estate in West Sussex. Drone footage, taken before the pair started sitting on them, showed three large eggs. The fact that they were infertile and did not hatch was not too disappointing. The pair are only four years old, and storks can live to over thirty, with their first attempts to breed often failing. Prospects for next year are encouraging. These young storks are part of a project to return the species to Britain, inspired by reintroductions in European countries that more than reached their target. Imported from Poland, they have spent the best part of three years in a six-acre pen with a group of other juveniles and several injured, non-flying adults, also from Poland. Other birds have already shown strong loyalty to the site. Two years ago, a young bird from Knepp flew across the Channel to France and, this summer, returned to its companions.

C In the face of reports of unrelenting ecological loss (the UN estimates a million species are on the brink of extinction globally), the white stork's return is refreshing news. As tens of thousands of people demonstrate about the growing climate crisis and eco-anxiety besets us, these glimpses of restoration are important. Featuring the storks in BBC television's *Springwatch* in June, the ecologist Chris Packham described the project as 'imaginative, intelligent, progressive and practical'.

D And yet its path to restoration in the UK has not been smooth. Support from conservation bodies has been surprisingly difficult to obtain; some were hard-pressed with their own initiatives, while others were simply reluctant to stick their necks out. In addition, the committee of the Sussex Wildlife Trust raised doubts about the stork ever having been a British bird. They also had concerns that English-bred birds would migrate across the Channel, and feared that their messy nests and closeness to humans would cause a hazard – rubbish falling down people's chimneys.

So how has the reintroduction project managed to get going? What makes it in some ways special is that it has had to rely on private individuals actually building the introduction pens themselves and feeding the birds at their own expense. The expertise of tiny yet determined conservation charities such as the Roy Dennis Wildlife Foundation – responsible for the successful reintroductions of ospreys and white-tailed eagles to Britain – has been very welcome. And the support of Cotswold Wildlife Park, which quarantined the original Polish birds and continues to manage and cover the costs of the captive-breeding programme using its own well-trained staff and excellent facilities, has proved invaluable.

E Across Europe, as stork populations have suffered from the draining of wetlands and disappearance of insect-rich pastures and meadows, their loss has been felt deeply. A few years ago, a tearful old woman in a village in Belarus showed me the nest on her roof, empty of storks for the first time in living memory. Where storks have been reintroduced, they are greeted with great happiness and some historical stork festivals have been restored. The Spanish erect poles for nests along their motorways, and in Alsace householders install cartwheels for storks to build nests on their roofs. During a cold snap in Bulgaria last March, villagers even gave white storks access to their homes.

F A driving motivation behind the project in the UK is the aspiration that the storks' return will spark feelings of empathy and affection from townspeople who see their nests on rooftops. They might also encourage the public to feel worried about the wider area where they fly off to feed on earthworms, grasshoppers and frogs. White storks could be that charismatic species that connects urban communities directly with landscape restoration. Certainly, people once loved them here. The name of our local village, Storrington, was originally 'Estorcheton' or 'home of the storks'. The public response has been overwhelming, with crowds coming to see white storks flying free in England for the first time in hundreds of years, and private landowners queueing up to offer more introduction sites.

The flight of the white stork over Britain is the triumph of practical action over bureaucracy, self-interest and negativity.

Questions 34–37

Complete the summary below.

Choose **ONE WORD ONLY** *from the text for each answer.*

Write your answers in boxes 34–37 on your answer sheet.

Project to reintroduce white storks at Knepp Estate

Last spring, two white storks were observed nesting at Knepp Estate, putting **34** .... together high up in a large oak tree. The female laid three eggs, which unfortunately proved to be **35** .... However, this was not surprising for such young storks. Naturalists believe they are likely to breed successfully in the future.

These two storks were bred in **36** .... and, after arriving in the UK, were kept for several years together with a few fully mature storks and some fellow juveniles before being released at Knepp. It appears that other storks are developing a sense of **37** .... to their new home. One left Knepp for a year, only to fly back to be with the group again.

Questions 38–40

*Choose the correct letter, **A**, **B**, **C** or **D**.*

Write the correct letter in boxes 38–40 on your answer sheet.

38 In Section A, we learn that in the past people thought white storks

A represented the deep snow and cold days of winter.
B had the power to ensure that babies were born safely.
C were a speciality that only the very rich were allowed to eat.
D might be used to encourage people to get rid of the monarchy.

39 The Sussex Wildlife Trust committee was unwilling to support the storks because

A it thought there might not be any safe breeding places locally.
B it worried whether they would survive in Britain long enough.
C it was unsure that they were actually a native species.
D it had too many other worthy projects to support.

40 What has been one effect of stork reintroductions in Europe?

A A variety of measures have been taken to create nesting sites.
B Changes have been made to the routes of some major roads.
C Special shelters have been made to protect the birds in bad weather.
D Some people have strengthened their roofs to support the birds' weight.

 → p. 124

WRITING

WRITING TASK 1

You should spend about 20 minutes on this task.

> ***Your English-speaking friend has asked for your help with a college project he/she is doing about celebrating New Year in different countries.***
>
> ***Write a letter to your friend. In your letter***
>
> - ***say how important New Year is to people in your country***
> - ***describe how New Year is celebrated in your country***
> - ***explain what you like about New Year celebrations in your country***

Write at least 150 words.

You do **NOT** need to write any addresses.

Begin your letter as follows:

Dear ………………………………,

→ p. 131

WRITING TASK 2

You should spend about 40 minutes on this task.

Write about the following topic:

Some people say that it is better to work for a large company than a small one.

Do you agree or disagree?

Give reasons for your answer and include any relevant examples from your own knowledge or experience.

Write at least 250 words.

→ p. 132

SPEAKING

PART 1

Example Speaking test video

The examiner asks you about yourself, your home, work or studies and other familiar topics.

EXAMPLE

Paying bills

- What kinds of bills do you have to pay?
- How do you usually pay your bills – in cash or by another method? [Why?]
- Have you ever forgotten to pay a bill? [Why/Why not?]
- Is there anything you could do to make your bills cheaper? [Why/Why not?]

PART 2

Describe some food or drink that you learned to prepare.

You should say:
what food or drink you learned to prepare
when and where you learned to prepare this
how you learned to prepare this

and explain how you felt about learning to prepare this food or drink.

You will have to talk about the topic for one to two minutes. You have one minute to think about what you are going to say. You can make some notes to help you if you wish.

PART 3

Discussion topics:

Young people and cooking

Example questions:
What kinds of things can children learn to cook?
Do you think it is important for children to learn to cook?
Do you think young people should learn to cook at home or at school?

Working as a chef

Example questions:
How enjoyable do you think it would be to work as a professional chef?
What skills does a person need to be a great chef?
How much influence do celebrity/TV chefs have on what ordinary people cook?

Test 2

LISTENING

PART 1 *Questions 1–10*

Questions 1–5

Complete the notes below.

Write **ONE WORD ONLY** *for each answer.*

Working at Milo's Restaurants

Benefits

- **1** .... provided for all staff
- **2** .... during weekdays at all Milo's Restaurants
- **3** .... provided after midnight

Person specification

- must be prepared to work well in a team
- must care about maintaining a high standard of **4** ....
- must have a qualification in **5** ....

Questions 6–10

Complete the table below.

Write ***ONE WORD AND/OR A NUMBER*** *for each answer.*

Location	Job title	Responsibilities include	Pay and conditions
6 …………… Street	Breakfast supervisor	Checking portions, etc. are correct Making sure **7** …………… is clean	Starting salary **8** £ …………… per hour Start work at 5.30 a.m.
City Road	Junior chef	Supporting senior chefs Maintaining stock and organising **9** ……………	Annual salary £23,000 No work on a **10** …………… once a month

→ p. 125 p. 108

PART 2 *Questions 11–20*

Questions 11 and 12

*Choose **TWO** letters, **A–E**.*

What are the **TWO** main reasons why this site has been chosen for the housing development?

A It has suitable geographical features.
B There is easy access to local facilities.
C It has good connections with the airport.
D The land is of little agricultural value.
E It will be convenient for workers.

Questions 13 and 14

*Choose **TWO** letters, **A–E**.*

Which **TWO** aspects of the planned housing development have people given positive feedback about?

A the facilities for cyclists
B the impact on the environment
C the encouragement of good relations between residents
D the low cost of all the accommodation
E the rural location

Questions 15–20

Label the map below.

*Write the correct letter, **A–I**, next to Questions 15–20.*

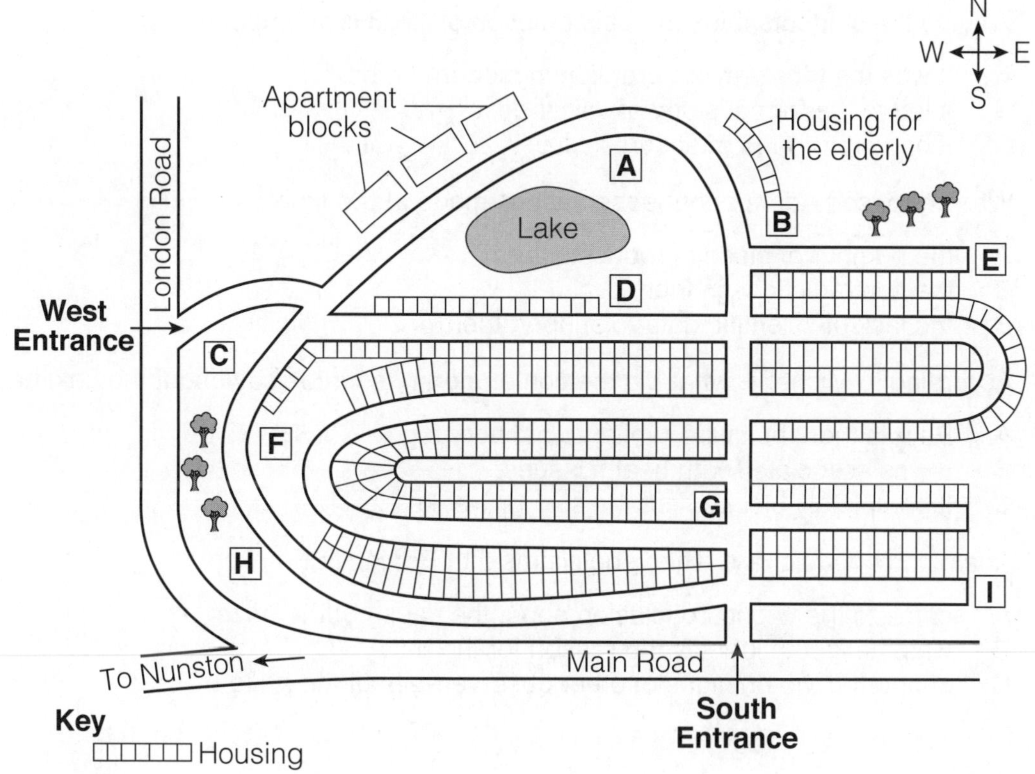

15 School ....

16 Sports centre ....

17 Clinic ....

18 Community centre ....

19 Supermarket ....

20 Playground ....

→ p. 125 p. 109

PART 3 *Questions 21–30*

Questions 21–24

*Choose the correct letter, **A**, **B** or **C**.*

21 Why do the students think the Laki eruption of 1783 is so important?

A It was the most severe eruption in modern times.
B It led to the formal study of volcanoes.
C It had a profound effect on society.

22 What surprised Adam about observations made at the time?

A the number of places producing them
B the contradictions in them
C the lack of scientific data to support them

23 According to Michelle, what did the contemporary sources say about the Laki haze?

A People thought it was similar to ordinary fog.
B It was associated with health issues.
C It completely blocked out the sun for weeks.

24 Adam corrects Michelle when she claims that Benjamin Franklin

A came to the wrong conclusion about the cause of the haze.
B was the first to identify the reason for the haze.
C supported the opinions of other observers about the haze.

Questions 25 and 26

*Choose **TWO** letters, **A–E**.*

Which **TWO** issues following the Laki eruption surprised the students?

A how widespread the effects were
B how long-lasting the effects were
C the number of deaths it caused
D the speed at which the volcanic ash cloud spread
E how people ignored the warning signs

Questions 27–30

What comment do the students make about the impact of the Laki eruption on the following countries?

*Choose **FOUR** answers from the box and write the correct letter, **A–F**, next to Questions 27–30.*

Comments

- **A** This country suffered the most severe loss of life.
- **B** The impact on agriculture was predictable.
- **C** There was a significant increase in deaths of young people.
- **D** Animals suffered from a sickness.
- **E** This country saw the highest rise in food prices in the world.
- **F** It caused a particularly harsh winter.

Countries

27 Iceland ....

28 Egypt ....

29 UK ....

30 USA ....

PART 4 *Questions 31–40*

Listening test audio

Complete the notes below.

Write ***ONE WORD ONLY*** *for each answer.*

Pockets

Reason for choice of subject

- They are **31** ……………………… but can be overlooked by consumers and designers.

Pockets in men's clothes

- Men started to wear **32** ……………………… in the 18th century.
- A **33** ……………………… sewed pockets into the lining of the garments.
- The wearer could use the pockets for small items.
- Bigger pockets might be made for men who belonged to a certain type of **34** ……………………… .

Pockets in women's clothes

- Women's pockets were less **35** ……………………… than men's.
- Women were very concerned about pickpockets.
- Pockets were produced in pairs using **36** ……………………… to link them together.
- Pockets hung from the women's **37** ……………………… under skirts and petticoats.
- Items such as **38** ……………………… could be reached through a gap in the material.
- Pockets, of various sizes, stayed inside clothing for many decades.
- When dresses changed shape, hidden pockets had a negative effect on the **39** ……………………… of women.
- Bags called 'pouches' became popular, before women carried a **40** ……………………… .

→ p. 125 p. 112

READING

SECTION 1 *Questions 1–14*

Read the text below and answer Questions 1–8.

Choosing the best sleeping bag

When choosing a sleeping bag, check what seasons it's for, as well as how heavy it is if you're backpacking. Also think about the filling. Natural duck down is very warm, has a longer lifespan and is easier to pack up, while synthetic materials are easier to clean, and they dry quicker and are cheaper.

A Vango Fuse -12

This all-year-round sleeping bag combines natural duck down and a new synthetic fibre. The result is a bag that's warm and weighs 1.5kg. There's a water-resistant finish to protect it from moisture.

B Outwell Campion Lux Double Sleeping Bag

This double sleeping bag – which is suitable for all seasons except winter – is soft and cosy, and there's a handy pocket for essentials, located inside near the top. It also folds up remarkably small, given its size.

C Nordisk Oscar +10

At just 350g, this sleeping bag is remarkably light, and as it's synthetic, it's very easy to maintain. The pack size is just 13×20cm, which makes it ideal for backpacking. It will work perfectly for summer trekking.

D The Big Sleep 250GSM Single Cowl Sleeping

If you want a no-frills, budget sleeping bag that will last more than one summer, opt for this. It's soft, comfy and simple to wash. Give yourself a bit of time to fit it back in the bag, though. Use it for spring, summer and autumn.

E Jack Wolfskin Smoozip +3

We like the extra insulation in this sleeping bag around the areas that tend to feel the cold (head, chest and feet). And the hood is cosy enough to use as a pillow.

F Vango Starwalker Dragon

This innovative, high-quality kids' sleeping bag enables you to undo some zips and turn it into a fun, animal-themed coat. Once your youngster is ready for bed, simply zip the bottom back on and zip up the shoulders. Suitable for between 8 and 20 degrees Celsius.

G Outwell Conqueror

This sleeping bag has an integrated down duvet and lots of space. What's more, it packs up compactly and is easy to get back in the bag. It's light but too big for a rucksack.

Questions 1–8

Look at the seven reviews of sleeping bags, ***A–G****, on pages 39 and 40.*

For which sleeping bag are the following statements true?

Write the correct letter, ***A–G****, in boxes 1–8 on your answer sheet.*

NB *You may use any letter more than once.*

1 This sleeping bag is not very easy to pack up.

2 People can use this sleeping bag in any season.

3 This sleeping bag has been designed to ensure certain parts of the body are warm.

4 This sleeping bag contains a useful storage area.

5 People who do not want to spend much on a sleeping bag will find this one suits their needs.

6 This sleeping bag can also keep the user warm during the daytime.

7 People who wish to avoid carrying heavy weights should try this sleeping bag.

8 This sleeping bag contains two different types of material.

Read the text below and answer Questions 9–14.

The Spread the Word Life Writing Prize

We are delighted to announce The Spread the Word Life Writing Prize in association with Goldsmiths Writers' Centre.

Competition Rules

Entries should be original works of life writing of no more than 5,000 words. The word count will be checked and entries longer than 5,000 words will be disqualified. There is no minimum word count.

For the purposes of the Prize, Life Writing is defined as non-fiction and should be based on a significant portion from the author's own experience. Traditional biographies, where the piece is only about the experience of someone else, are excluded.

Writers only submit one entry each. Multiple entries by the same author will result in only the first entry being considered for the Prize and any additional entries disqualified. Writers who have previously won or been highly commended in the Life Writing Prize are excluded from entering; otherwise, previous entrants may submit.

Entries must be the original, previously unpublished work of the entrant. Graphic novel-style entries, where drawings or photographs accompany text, are welcome. Entries can be self-contained pieces of life writing, or the first 5,000 words of a longer piece of work.

The Life Writing Prize is open to writers aged over 18 and resident in the UK who are emerging writers, which means they have not previously published in print a full-length work. We define a full-length work as, for example, a complete work of fiction or non-fiction over 30,000 words.

Entries that are simultaneously submitted elsewhere are welcome – but please let us know as soon as possible if a piece is to be published elsewhere or has won another prize so we can disqualify it from the Life Writing Prize.

The winner will receive £1,500, publication on Spread the Word's website, two years' membership of the Royal Society of Literature, and a development meeting with an editor and an agent. Two highly commended entries will receive £500 and two mentoring sessions, a development meeting with an editor and an agent, and be published on the Spread the Word website.

Questions 9–14

Do the following statements agree with the information given in the text on page 42?

In boxes 9–14 on your answer sheet, write

TRUE *if the statement agrees with the information*
FALSE *if the statement contradicts the information*
NOT GIVEN *if there is no information on this*

9 Writers can submit an entry of fewer than 5,000 words for the Life Writing Prize.

10 Writers can choose to write about the life of a person they know.

11 People who have entered an earlier Life Writing competition without achieving any success may enter again.

12 Writers who are between 19 and 25 years old and in full-time education have won the prize in previous years.

13 Only one prize is awarded at the end of the Life Writing competition.

14 Previous winners of the Life Writing Prize have gone on to become successful published writers.

→ p. 126

SECTION 2 *Questions 15–27*

Read the text below and answer Questions 15–21.

Encouraging employees to be healthy: a guide for employers

Benefits

Putting effort into employee wellness can reduce absenteeism and encourage better teamwork in the workplace, as well as increased productivity. Once you've devised a program, continue to assess the outcomes and regularly survey your team to gather feedback.

Focus on general prevention

Consider offering flu vaccinations on site and look at offering employees incentives on health insurance. Some companies arrange for someone who specialises in health issues, such as a doctor, to visit the workplace and speak to employees.

Encourage a healthier diet

Most of us know that eating healthily can help prevent future diseases, but many are not aware that unhealthy eating is linked to a 66 percent increased risk of loss of productivity. It may be necessary to consciously develop a healthy food and drink workplace policy, including a healthy catering policy. A simple thing to do is substitute soda in any on-site vending machines with water or juice. Also investigate the nutritional value of food supplied for team meetings and work events. Consider putting a bowl of fruit out in the staff room and urge everyone to help themselves for free. You can encourage employees to bring in healthy lunches from home by making sure that there is a fridge in the break room.

Encourage more exercise

Encouraging employees to exercise needn't be expensive as there are plenty of low-cost methods available. These might include: installing racks for bikes in your staff car park; encouraging employees to take part in fun runs and charity events; suggesting 'walking meetings' where people discuss business as they get fresh air and exercise; and putting in showers to assist those who ride or run to the workplace. Some companies negotiate group rates for their employees at a nearby gym.

Improve mental health

Recent reports have shown that ignoring mental health costs Australian companies at least $11 billion a year. We all have a responsibility to look out for one another. Some ways you can do this in the workplace include: running employee surveys to get valuable information on morale in the workplace; training managers on mental health strategies; offering rebates so employees are compensated for counselling if required; and refusing to accept any bullying and unprofessional behaviour in your workplace.

Questions 15–21

Complete the notes below.

Choose **ONE WORD ONLY** *from the text for each answer.*

Write your answers in boxes 15–21 on your answer sheet.

Encouraging employee health

Benefits

- improved efficiency
- less **15** ....

Preventing problems

- invite guests, e.g., a doctor, to give information
- provide vaccinations

Diet

- make healthier options available to replace **16** ....
- have healthy food at meetings
- offer **17** .... at no cost
- provide a **18** .... for staff use

Exercise

- provide somewhere for employees to leave their **19** ....
- provide **20** .... for workers who exercise

Mental health

- give managers appropriate training
- find out how employees feel at work by using **21** ....
- do not tolerate bullying or other inappropriate behaviour

Read the text below and answer Questions 22–27.

Marama Beach Hotel and Bistro: guidelines for working in the kitchen

The health and well-being of customers and staff is our first priority, and we expect all staff to take every step possible to maintain food safety and work in a hygienic manner.

Hygiene

- Long hair must be tied back and no rings may be worn if touching food.
- The regulation chefs' shirts and trousers are to be freshly laundered before starting a new shift, along with aprons if they are worn.
- Cross-contamination between raw and cooked food must be avoided. To this end, staff must use a clean board each time they cut different types of food.
- Staff should not touch money and then food without washing their hands in between.
- In the case of illness or a skin problem, the staff member should inform the manager. Cuts on hands and arms must be properly wrapped or bandaged.

Safety rules

- All injuries must be reported to management immediately.
- Safety guards must not be altered in any way, and staff must always wear protective clothing and gloves when working with sharp, hot, cold or corrosive items or materials.
- Loose clothing or jewellery must not be worn.
- Defective appliances must be turned off and not used – staff must not try to fix them themselves.
- Heavy boxes should be lifted carefully with bent knees and a straight back, holding the box close to the body.
- Work areas should be clean and free of hazards.
- Spills on the floor must be dealt with immediately.
- Flammable liquids must be stored away from flames.
- If storing containers of chemicals in the kitchen, they must have clear labels, so as to avoid any confusion about the contents.

Breaks

Staff have 20 minutes of paid break time per 3 hours of work, during which time they may not leave the premises. Every staff member who works a shift exceeding 5 hours is entitled to a 30-minute unpaid break and free meals. However, please be aware that the kitchen may not always be able to provide this service, especially in peak times. Beverages kept in the storeroom may not be consumed by staff, but filtered water is provided free of charge in the staff room.

Questions 22–27

Complete the sentences below.

Choose **ONE WORD ONLY** *from the text for each answer.*

Write your answers in boxes 22–27 on your answer sheet.

22 Chefs' uniforms and .... must be washed for every shift.

23 Kitchen staff need to change the .... when they start chopping another kind of food.

24 All staff must make sure their hands are clean after handling ....

25 Workers in the kitchen should not attempt to repair ....

26 .... are required to identify any chemicals kept in the kitchen.

27 It is forbidden for kitchen staff to have drinks from the ....

 → p. 126

SECTION 3 *Questions 28–40*

Read the text below and answer Questions 28–40.

A home-sewing revival: the return of Clothkits

In the 1970s, Clothkits revolutionised home sewing. Later, a woman from Sussex, England, revived the nostalgic brand and brought it up to date

A 'I can't remember many of the clothes I wore before I was six, but I have a vivid memory of a certain skirt whose patterns I can still trace in my mind. It was wraparound, with a belt that threaded through itself, decorated with cats in two shades of green. I wore it with a knitted red jersey my mum bought in a jumble sale, and brown sandals with flowers cut into the toes. It was 1979, and I was not yet five. I forgot about that skirt for a long time, but when a girlfriend mentioned the name Clothkits while we were chatting, it was as if a door suddenly opened on a moment in the past that resonated with vivid significance for me.' The brand, founded in 1968, had by the late 1980s mostly vanished from people's lives, but by a combination of determination and luck Kay Mawer brought it back.

B Clothkits was created by the designer Anne Kennedy, who came up with the ingenious idea of printing a pattern straight on to coloured fabric so that a paper pattern was not needed. It was accompanied by instructions that almost anyone could follow on how to cut the pieces out and sew them together. 'I was rebelling against the formulaic lines of textile design at that time,' Kennedy says. 'My interest was in folk art and clothes that were simple to make as I had lots of unfinished sewing disasters in my cupboard.' Clothkits has always embodied the spirit of the late 1960s and 1970s. Its initial design was a dress in a geometric stripe in orange, pink, turquoise and purple. It cost 25 shillings (£1.25), and after it was featured in the *Observer* newspaper, Kennedy received more than £2,000 worth of orders. She ran the company from Lewes in Sussex, where at its peak it employed more than 400 people, selling to 44 countries worldwide. Sew-your-own kits formed the core of the business, supplemented by knitwear. Kennedy's children demonstrated the patterns by wearing them in photographs.

C Kennedy sold the company in the late 1980s. There had been a few administrative problems with postal strikes and a new computer system, which back then took up an entire room, 'but the times were changing as well,' she says. 'More women were going out to work and sewing less for their children.' She sold the company to one of her suppliers, who then sold it on to Freeman's, which ran Clothkits alongside its own brand for a while, using Kennedy's impressive database, but its ethos as a big, corporate company did not sit well alongside the alternative and artistic values of Clothkits. In 1991, Clothkits was made dormant, and there the story might have ended, were it not for Mawer's fascination with discovering what happened to Clothkits.

D Mawer's mother bought her a sewing machine when she was ten and taught her basic pattern-cutting and garment construction, encouraging her to experiment with colour and design by trial and error. The first garment Mawer made was a pair of trousers, which she made by tracing around an existing pair of trousers. In her late twenties, she spent five years working on digital and sculptural installations. 'It was an amazing, mind-expanding experience, but I knew it was unlikely I could make a living as a practising artist. I was definitely looking for a way that I could work in a creative industry with a commercial edge.' The experience inspired Mawer to return to education, studying for a degree in fine art at the University of Chichester. Her passion for vintage fabric, which her mother had encouraged her to start collecting, led her back to Clothkits, and from there to a journey into the heart of Freeman's. Negotiations with the company took 18 months, but in October 2007 Clothkits was hers.

E The ethos of Clothkits remains the same, and Mawer is proud that her fabric is printed either in London or the north of England, and that packaging is kept to an absolute minimum. 'I wanted to feel that everyone involved in the brand, from design to production, was part of a process I could witness. I couldn't see the point of manufacturing on the other side of the world, as that's not what Clothkits has ever been about.' The revival of Clothkits has also, of course, coincided with a growing sense of dissatisfaction at our disposable society, and the resulting resurgence of interest in skills such as sewing and knitting. 'Making your own clothes gives you a greater appreciation of the craftsmanship in the construction of a garment,' Mawer says. 'When you know the process involved in making a skirt, you treasure it in a way you wouldn't if you'd bought it from a mass-producing manufacturer.'

Questions 28–31

The text on pages 49 and 50 has five paragraphs, **A–E**.

Which paragraph mentions the following?

Write the correct letter, ***A–E****, in boxes 28–31 on your answer sheet.*

NB *You may use any letter more than once.*

28 mention of Mawer's desire to oversee all the stages of her business

29 reference to changing employment patterns among the general population

30 the date when Clothkits was originally established as a product

31 the benefits of sewing a garment and then wearing it

Questions 32–35

*Choose the correct letter, **A**, **B**, **C** or **D**.*

Write the correct letter in boxes 32–35 on your answer sheet.

32 In Paragraph A, the writer says that Kay Mawer was reminded about Clothkits by

A a shop she visited.
B a purchase she made.
C an outfit someone was wearing.
D a conversation with someone she knew.

33 What does the reader learn about Clothkits in the 1960s and 1970s?

A Its designs represented the attitudes of the time.
B Its products were only affordable for the wealthy.
C Its creator tried many times to launch her company.
D Its management was spread across numerous countries.

34 Why did Clothkits close in 1991?

A There were unexpected staffing problems.
B The funding for sewing activities was inadequate.
C Freeman's was an unsuitable partner.
D Records on Kennedy's database were lost.

35 What point does the writer make in Paragraph E?

A Clothkits will reach more markets than in the past.
B Clothkits will need bigger premises than in the past.
C People are more concerned about throwing away items than in the past.
D People do less sewing now than in the past.

Questions 36–40

Complete the summary below.

*Choose **ONE WORD ONLY** from the text for each answer.*

Write your answers in boxes 36–40 on your answer sheet.

The early days of Clothkits

Clothkits was started by a designer named Anne Kennedy. Her clothing company specialised in selling **36** .... with a pattern printed on it. This came with **37** .... , which meant that buyers were able to make their own garments.

The very first garment Anne Kennedy made was a multi-coloured striped dress with a **38** .... pattern. A **39** .... article led to many orders for this from around the world. As the company grew, she increased her workforce, and also sold **40** .... as part of her business. She exhibited her designs using her children as models.

→ p. 126

WRITING

WRITING TASK 1

You should spend about 20 minutes on this task.

You are soon going to spend three months doing work experience in an organisation.

Write a letter to the manager of the organisation where you are going to do work experience. In your letter

- ***thank the manager for the opportunity to do work experience***
- ***explain what you hope to learn from the work experience***
- ***ask some questions about the work experience you are going to do***

Write at least 150 words.

You do **NOT** need to write any addresses.

Begin your letter as follows:

Dear Sir or Madam,

 → p. 133

WRITING TASK 2

You should spend about 40 minutes on this task.

Write about the following topic:

When we meet someone for the first time, we generally decide very quickly what kind of person we think they are and if we like them or not.

Is this a good thing or a bad thing?

Give reasons for your answer and include any relevant examples from your own knowledge or experience.

Write at least 250 words.

→ p. 134

SPEAKING

PART 1

The examiner asks you about yourself, your home, work or studies and other familiar topics.

EXAMPLE

Science

- Did you like studying science when you were at school? [Why/Why not?]
- What do you remember about your science teachers at school?
- How interested are you in science now? [Why/Why not?]
- What do you think has been an important recent scientific development? [Why?]

PART 2

Describe a tourist attraction in your country that you would recommend.

You should say:
what the tourist attraction is
where in your country this tourist attraction is
what visitors can see and do at this tourist attraction
and explain why you would recommend this tourist attraction.

You will have to talk about the topic for one to two minutes. You have one minute to think about what you are going to say. You can make some notes to help you if you wish.

PART 3

Discussion topics:

Museums and art galleries

Example questions:
What are the most popular museums and art galleries in … / where you live?
Do you believe that all museums and art galleries should be free?
What kinds of things make a museum or art gallery an interesting place to visit?

The holiday industry

Example questions:
Why, do you think, do some people book package holidays rather than travelling independently?
Would you say that large numbers of tourists cause problems for local people?
What sort of impact can large holiday resorts have on the environment?

Test 3

LISTENING

Listening test audio

PART 1 ***Questions 1–10***

Questions 1–4

Complete the form below.

Write ***ONE WORD AND/OR A NUMBER*** *for each answer.*

Wayside Camera Club membership form	
Name:	Dan Green
Email address:	dan1068@market.com
Home address:	52 **1** ……………… Street, Peacetown
Heard about us:	from a **2** ………………
Reasons for joining:	to enter competitions to **3** ………………
Type of membership:	**4** ……………… membership (£30)

Questions 5–10

Complete the table below.

Write ***NO MORE THAN TWO WORDS*** *for each answer.*

Photography competitions		
Title of competition	**Instructions**	**Feedback to Dan**
5 '………………'	A scene in the home	The picture's composition was not good.
'Beautiful Sunsets'	Scene must show some **6** ………………	The **7** ……………… was wrong.
8 '………………'	Scene must show **9** ………………	The photograph was too **10** ……………… .

PART 2 *Questions 11–20*

Questions 11 and 12

*Choose **TWO** letters, **A–E**.*

Which **TWO** warnings does Dan give about picking mushrooms?

A Don't pick more than one variety of mushroom at a time.
B Don't pick mushrooms near busy roads.
C Don't eat mushrooms given to you.
D Don't eat mushrooms while picking them.
E Don't pick old mushrooms.

Questions 13 and 14

*Choose **TWO** letters, **A–E**.*

Which **TWO** ideas about wild mushrooms does Dan say are correct?

A Mushrooms should always be peeled before eating.
B Mushrooms eaten by animals may be unsafe.
C Cooking destroys toxins in mushrooms.
D Brightly coloured mushrooms can be edible.
E All poisonous mushrooms have a bad smell.

Questions 15–20

Choose the correct letter, ***A***, ***B*** *or* ***C***.

15 What advice does Dan give about picking mushrooms in parks?

A Choose wooded areas.
B Don't disturb wildlife.
C Get there early.

16 Dan says it is a good idea for beginners to

A use a mushroom app.
B join a group.
C take a reference book.

17 What does Dan say is important for conservation?

A selecting only fully grown mushrooms
B picking a limited amount of mushrooms
C avoiding areas where rare mushroom species grow

18 According to Dan, some varieties of wild mushrooms are in decline because there is

A a huge demand for them from restaurants.
B a lack of rain in this part of the country.
C a rise in building developments locally.

19 Dan says that when storing mushrooms, people should

A keep them in the fridge for no more than two days.
B keep them in a brown bag in a dark room.
C leave them for a period after washing them.

20 What does Dan say about trying new varieties of mushrooms?

A Experiment with different recipes.
B Expect some to have a strong taste.
C Cook them for a long time.

→ p. 127 p. 114

PART 3 *Questions 21–30*

Questions 21 and 22

*Choose **TWO** letters, **A–E**.*

Which **TWO** opinions about the Luddites do the students express?

A Their actions were ineffective.
B They are still influential today.
C They have received unfair criticism.
D They were proved right.
E Their attitude is understandable.

Questions 23 and 24

*Choose **TWO** letters, **A–E**.*

Which **TWO** predictions about the future of work are the students doubtful about?

A Work will be more rewarding.
B Unemployment will fall.
C People will want to delay retiring.
D Working hours will be shorter.
E People will change jobs more frequently.

Questions 25–30

What comment do the students make about each of the following jobs?

*Choose **SIX** answers from the box and write the correct letter, **A–G**, next to Questions 25–30.*

Comments

A These jobs are likely to be at risk.

B Their role has become more interesting in recent years.

C The number of people working in this sector has fallen dramatically.

D This job will require more qualifications.

E Higher disposable income has led to a huge increase in jobs.

F There is likely to be a significant rise in demand for this service.

G Both employment and productivity have risen.

Jobs

25 Accountants ....

26 Hairdressers ....

27 Administrative staff ....

28 Agricultural workers ....

29 Care workers ....

30 Bank clerks ....

→ p. 127 p. 115

PART 4 *Questions 31–40*

Listening test audio

Complete the notes below.

Write ***ONE WORD ONLY*** *for each answer.*

Space Traffic Management

A Space Traffic Management system

- is a concept similar to Air Traffic Control, but for satellites rather than planes.
- would aim to set up legal and **31** .... ways of improving safety.
- does not actually exist at present.

Problems in developing effective Space Traffic Management

- Satellites are now quite **32** .... and therefore more widespread (e.g. there are constellations made up of **33** .... of satellites).
- At present, satellites are not required to transmit information to help with their **34** ....
- There are few systems for **35** .... satellites.
- Small pieces of debris may be difficult to identify.
- Operators may be unwilling to share details of satellites used for **36** .... or commercial reasons.
- It may be hard to collect details of the object's **37** .... at a given time.
- Scientists can only make a **38** .... about where the satellite will go.

Solutions

- Common standards should be agreed on for the presentation of information.
- The information should be combined in one **39** ....
- A coordinated system must be designed to create **40** .... in its users.

 → p. 127 p. 117

READING

SECTION 1 *Questions 1–14*

Read the text below and answer Questions 1–7.

Manly Beaches

Next time you visit Manly, 30 minutes by ferry from the centre of Australia's biggest city, Sydney, try some of these less famous beaches

A Fairy Bower

Located in a marine protection area, the water is perfect for paddling, snorkelling or even scuba diving. There is a small gift shop for unusual souvenirs, and a kiosk that rents stand-up paddleboards. Buses do not stop nearby so a walk is necessary.

B North Steyne

This popular beach is a little further from the ferry than the main beach and it always feels less crowded. North Steyne has professional lifeguards on duty, but the surf can be hazardous so check conditions if swimming with young ones. If you want to try surfing for the first time, Manly Surf School operates out of the surf club located on the beach. Please note that boards are reserved for students and are not available for rent.

C Delwood

Delwood's secluded cove is a scenic walk from the ferry along the harbour walkway. There are no shops, so bring a picnic and have a peaceful swim off the rocks. You'll probably have the beach to yourself.

D Little Manly

This popular harbour beach has a net that encloses the swimming area. It is a good option for families as the protected area makes it easy to keep an eye on kids playing in the water. There is also a large playground, a public barbecue that anyone can use and toilet facilities, which make this a great spot for a family day out.

E East Esplanade

Located next to Manly Wharf, East Esplanade is a popular spot all day. There is no beach closer to the ferry or buses than this one. Kayakers meet for a paddle here as the sun rises, and daytrippers sit on the sand during the day. People get together on the grass after work, and bring drinks, snacks and music to watch the sun go down.

F Shelly Beach

This is the best spot if you don't like big waves. Rent a beach chair or head straight to the Boathouse Café, the perfect place for breakfast or lunch. Please note that Shelly Beach gets overly crowded at times, so avoid it on a sunny weekend afternoon.

Questions 1–7

*Look at the six beach descriptions, **A–F**, on pages 63 and 64.*

For which beaches are the following statements true?

*Write the correct letter, **A–F**, in boxes 1–7 on your answer sheet.*

NB *You may use any letter more than once.*

1 You can buy food at this beach.

2 You can learn to do a sport at this beach.

3 This beach can be uncomfortably busy.

4 Adults can supervise their children without much difficulty at this beach.

5 This beach is nearest to public transport.

6 People are employed to supervise swimmers at this beach.

7 You can hire sports equipment at this beach.

Read the text below and answer Questions 8–14.

Sydney Water: advice for customers paying a bill

About your bill

Sydney Water services over five million people in greater Sydney, and if you own a property, you'll get a bill from us. Generally, this is just for your water and wastewater services, but there could be other charges. We send most bills quarterly, after we've read the meter. If your property has no meter, we send the bill at the start of each quarter.

When do we send the bill?

If you'd like monthly bills, simply ask us to read your meter monthly. It costs $32.52 a quarter to be billed this way and this additional fee will appear on the first bill each quarter. To arrange it, just call us on 13 20 92.

What if you can't pay the bill?

We understand that it might be hard to pay your bill. If you're having difficulties, we have a range of options to help. If you receive a pension, we may give you a reduction on your bill, but you must own and live in your home to qualify for this.

How can you get your billing history?

- **Register for eBill.** When you register for Sydney Water's online billing facility, eBill, you'll be able to see your past bills at any time. Once you're registered, you'll stop getting paper bills and start getting electronic ones.
- **Still want paper bills?** Simply cancel your registration after you have saved the electronic bills you need. Then you'll go back to paper bills, but you won't have access to the online bills after you cancel.
- **Contact us.** Simply contact us and we'll give you a statement that shows the amounts we charged you and the payments we received on your last five bills.
- **Need more history?** If you need information that's older than your last five bills, you need to pay $28.04 for a 'billing record search statement'.

How do you stop a charge on a bill?

We'll stop a fixed charge on your bill if a licensed plumber cuts off your water or wastewater service. Your plumber must apply for this disconnection and follow Sydney Water's standard procedures.

Questions 8–14

Do the following statements agree with the information given in the text on page 66?

In boxes 8–14 on your answer sheet, write

TRUE	*if the statement agrees with the information*
FALSE	*if the statement contradicts the information*
NOT GIVEN	*if there is no information on this*

8 All property owners receive Sydney Water bills.

9 Customers who don't have a water meter must pay an extra charge.

10 Customers who choose to receive a bill every month pay extra.

11 Pensioners who live in rented accommodation might get a discount.

12 Customers registered for eBill receive both paper and electronic bills.

13 Customers who request information from the period before their last five bills must pay a fee.

14 A fixed charge can be avoided when the water supply is disconnected by a licensed plumber.

→ p. 128

SECTION 2 *Questions 15–27*

Read the text below and answer Questions 15–20.

Company car parking policy

DG Contracts recognises that many people working in the organisation require a vehicle for business purposes and aims to provide parking facilities for as many individuals as possible. However, car parking provision is limited. DG Contracts therefore actively encourages staff to reduce their carbon footprint by using public transport, walking or cycling, or by organising ways of sharing the use of cars.

The car parking policy aims to allocate parking on a fair and equitable basis with spaces being given first to those employees who claim above a certain mileage of travel for business purposes. Individuals who are allocated a parking space will be issued with a parking permit and a number which corresponds to a car parking space. If there are any non-allocated car parking spaces, these can be utilised by employees on a first-come, first-served basis. In some cases, designated parking areas are required for company vehicles, which must be parked securely at night. However, employees may park in these areas in the daytime.

If any individual leaves the company prior to the expiry of their parking permit, this will be handed on to the member of staff who acts as their replacement, assuming that this person requires it. If any individual who has been issued a parking permit takes maternity leave or is signed off work for a lengthy period, their parking permit will be re-allocated to the staff member appointed as cover for this individual during their absence.

Employees who park their cars in a DG company car park do so at their own risk and must follow the rules laid down in the parking policy. If you have any complaints concerning any aspect of car parking at DG company car parks, please address them to the HR Manager.

Questions 15–20

Complete the sentences below.

*Choose **ONE WORD ONLY** from the text for each answer.*

Write your answers in boxes 15–20 on your answer sheet.

15 Parking is limited, so the use of alternative methods of transport and the .... of cars is encouraged.

16 Staff with the highest .... are given parking spaces first.

17 Some parking spaces are reserved for company vehicles during the .... but may be used by staff at other times.

18 If an employee leaves the company permanently, their parking space will normally be given to their ....

19 If an employee takes extended leave, their parking space will be given to the person who provides .... for the absent employee.

20 All .... about car parking should be sent to the HR Manager.

Read the text below and answer Questions 21–27.

Ensuring safety in the office

It's fairly obvious that safety and health hazards can exist on worksites filled with heavy machinery and equipment. However, a surprising number of hazards can also be present in the office.

The most common types of injuries are slips, trips and falls. Boxes, files and other items piled in walkways can create a tripping hazard. Be certain that all materials are safely stored in their proper location to prevent build-up of clutter. Further, in addition to posing an electrical hazard, stretching wires across walkways creates a tripping hazard, so ensure they are properly secured and covered.

Standing on rolling office chairs is a significant fall hazard. Workers who need to reach something at an elevated height should use a stepladder, which must be fully opened and placed on level ground.

Workers can collide when making turns in the hallways and around blind corners. This can be prevented by installing mirrors in these places so workers can see who is coming. Floors may also present a hazard. Marble or tile can become very slippery, particularly when wet. The use of carpets can help to reduce falls and can be especially helpful at main doors, where workers are likely to be coming in with wet shoes.

Another type of injury comes from workers being struck by an object. Filing cabinets may be in danger of tipping over if drawers are left open, and filing cabinets and desks may also create a tripping hazard if they are not properly closed. High piles of materials and equipment can cause major injuries if they are knocked over. Heavy objects should always be stored close to the ground, and the load capacity of shelves should never be exceeded.

Because office workers spend most of their day seated at a desk, they are prone to strains and other injuries related to posture and repetitive movement. Desks, seating, monitor stands, etc. should all be adjustable in order to accommodate the widest possible range of employees. Typing from hard copy can lead to neck strain if a worker is forced to look down repeatedly to the desk at the document being copied and back to the computer screen. This can be prevented by providing holders, which help to prevent muscle imbalance by positioning the document at the same level as the screen. Another cause of neck injuries is incorrect placement of the computer mouse – this should always be kept beside the keyboard, and at the same level.

Questions 21–27

Complete the notes below.

Choose ***ONE WORD ONLY*** *from the text for each answer.*

Write your answers in boxes 21–27 on your answer sheet.

Making sure offices are safe

To prevent slips, trips, falls and collisions, ensure that

- boxes, files, etc. are correctly stored
- items such as **21** .... do not create a tripping hazard
- workers do not use **22** .... to reach high objects
- **23** .... are fixed at corners
- floors are covered by **24** .... , especially at entrances

To prevent injuries caused by objects, ensure that

- **25** .... in office furniture are kept closed
- objects which are heavy are kept near the floor

To prevent injuries due to posture and repetitive movement, ensure that

- office furniture is **26** ....
- **27** .... are provided for documents
- the mouse is placed next to the computer keyboard

→ p. 128

SECTION 3 *Questions 28–40*

Read the text below and answer Questions 28–40.

Roman Roads

A The long straight roads built by the Romans have, in many cases, become just as famous in history as their greatest emperors and generals. Building upon more ancient routes and creating a huge number of new ones, Roman engineers were fearless in their plans to join one point to another in as straight a line as possible, whatever the difficulties in geography and the costs in manpower. Consequently, roads required bridges, tunnels, viaducts and many other architectural and engineering features to create a series of breathtaking but highly useful monuments, which spread from Europe to eastern parts of the Roman empire.

B The Romans did not invent roads, but, as in so many other areas, they took an idea which went back as far as the Bronze Age and extended that concept, daring to squeeze from it the fullest possible potential. The first and most famous great Roman road was the *Via Appia*, or Appian Way. Constructed from 312 BCE, and covering 196 kilometres, it linked Rome to ancient Capua in Italy in as straight a line as possible and was appropriately known to the Romans as the *Regina Viarum* or 'Queen of Roads'. Much like a modern highway, it bypassed small towns along the way, and it largely ignored geographical obstacles. The road would later be extended to 569 kilometres in length.

C The network of public Roman roads covered over 120,000 kilometres. Besides permitting the rapid deployment of troops and, more importantly, the wheeled vehicles which supplied them with food and equipment, Roman roads allowed for an increase in trade and cultural exchange. Roads were also one of the ways Rome could demonstrate its authority. For this reason, many roads began and ended in a triumphal arch, and the imperial prestige associated with a road project was demonstrated in the fact that roads were very often named after the officials who funded them; for example, the *Via Appia* takes its name from the Roman magistrate Appius Claudius Caecus.

D To achieve the objective of constructing the shortest routes possible between two points, all manner of engineering difficulties had to be overcome. Once extensive surveying had been carried out, to ensure the proposed route was actually straight and to determine what various engineering methods were needed, marshes had to be drained, forests cut through, creeks diverted, bedrock channelled, mountainsides cut into, rivers crossed with bridges, valleys traversed with viaducts and tunnels built through mountains. When all that was done, roads had to be levelled, reinforced with support walls or terracing and then, of course, maintained, which they were for over 800 years.

E Major roads were around a standard 4.2 metres wide, which was enough space for two vehicles to pass each other. First a trench was dug in the earth, and a layer of large stones was used to form the foundation. This was followed by a substantial deposit of smaller broken materials – often crushed brick was used for this purpose, and on top of this, a layer of fine gravel was added. This upper section of the road was referred to as the nucleus and was then surfaced with blocks or slabs. Mountain roads might also have ridges running across the surface of the slabs, to give animals better grip, and have ruts cut into the stone to guide wheeled vehicles.

Roads were purposely inclined slightly from the centre down to the kerb to allow rainwater to run off along the sides. Many also had parallel ditches that collected the runoff and formed a drainage canal on each side of the road. A path of packed gravel for pedestrians typically ran along each side of the road, varying in width from 1 to 3 metres. Separating the path from the road were the kerb stones, which were regular upright slabs. Busier stretches of main roads had areas where vehicles could pull over, and some of these had services for travellers and their animals. Milestones were also set up at regular intervals along the road and these often recorded who was responsible for the upkeep of that stretch of the road and what repairs had been made.

F Lasting symbols of the imagination of Roman engineers are the many arched bridges and viaducts still standing today that helped achieve the engineers' straight-line goal. The Romans built to last, and the piers of bridges which crossed rivers, for example, were often built with a resistant prow-shape and used massive durable blocks of stone, while the upper parts might be built of stone blocks strengthened with iron clamps. Perhaps the most impressive bridge was at Narni; 180 metres long, 8 metres wide and as high as 33 metres, it had 4 massive semicircular arches, one of which, stretching 32.1 metres, ranks as one of the longest block-arch spans in the ancient world. Recently hit by earthquakes, it is now having to undergo restoration work to repair the effects.

Such was the engineering and surveying skill of the Romans that many of their roads have provided the basis for hundreds of today's routes across Europe and the Middle East. Many roads in Italy still use the original Roman name for certain stretches, and some bridges, such as at Tre Ponti in Venice, still carry road traffic today.

Questions 28–33

The text on pages 72 and 73 has six sections, **A–F**.

Which section mentions the following?

*Write the correct letter, **A–F**, in boxes 28–33 on your answer sheet.*

NB *You may use any letter more than once.*

28 the various functions of Roman roads

29 reference to some current remains of Roman road building

30 a description of preparations for building a road

31 the period in history when road building began

32 the consequence of damage caused by a natural disaster

33 the total distance once crossed by Roman roads

Questions 34–37

Choose the correct letter, ***A****,* ***B****,* ***C*** *or* ***D****.*

Write the correct letter in boxes 34–37 on your answer sheet.

34 Which aspect of Roman road building does the writer mention in Section A?

A the strength and permanence of the roads
B the magnificence and practicality of the roads
C the number of people involved in building
D the powerful people who financed the roads

35 The writer compares the Appian Way to a modern highway because

A it was lengthened over time.
B it took a long time to construct.
C It was used by a large number of travellers.
D it was designed to avoid certain areas.

36 According to the writer, the purpose of the triumphal arches was to

A display the power of Rome.
B celebrate the opening of a road.
C show the name of important roads.
D provide access for important officials.

37 What common use of a milestone is mentioned in Section E?

A indicating to travellers the total length of the road
B highlighting areas of the road that needed repair
C noting details regarding the maintenance of the road
D marking rest places along the road for travellers and their animals

Questions 38–40

Label the diagram below.

Choose ***NO MORE THAN TWO WORDS*** *from the text for each answer.*

Write your answers in boxes 38–40 on your answer sheet.

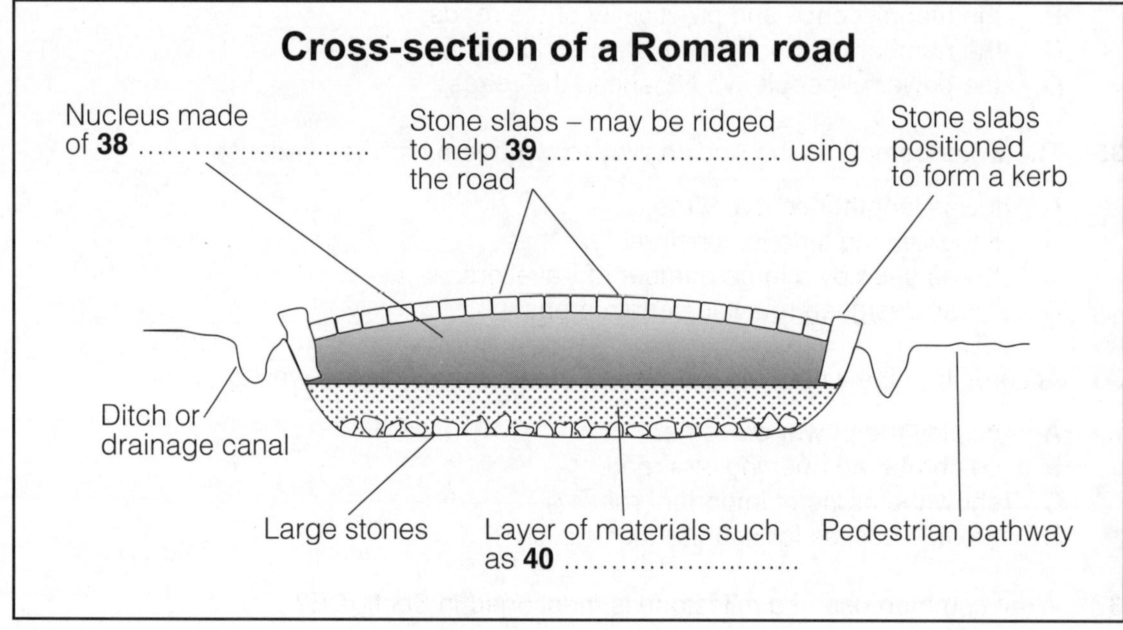

 → p. 128

WRITING TASK 1

You should spend about 20 minutes on this task.

You recently bought some train tickets for a journey a week in advance. When you went to the station to catch the train, you were told you could not use the tickets and the staff were very unhelpful to you.

Write a letter to the train company. In your letter

- ***describe the problem you had with the tickets***
- ***say why you were unhappy with the staff***
- ***suggest what action the train company should take***

Write at least 150 words.

You do **NOT** need to write any addresses.

Begin your letter as follows:

Dear Sir or Madam,

→ p. 135

WRITING TASK 2

You should spend about 40 minutes on this task.

Write about the following topic:

In the past, most working people had only one job. However, nowadays, more and more people have more than one job at the same time.

What are the reasons for this development?

What are the advantages and disadvantages of having more than one job?

Give reasons for your answer and include any relevant examples from your own knowledge or experience.

Write at least 250 words.

 → p. 136

SPEAKING

PART 1

The examiner asks you about yourself, your home, work or studies and other familiar topics.

EXAMPLE

Online shopping

- How often do you buy things online? [Why?]
- What was the last thing you bought online?
- Do you ever see things in shops and then buy them online? [Why/Why not?]
- Do you think the popularity of online shopping is changing your town or city centre? [Why/Why not?]

PART 2

Describe a time when you enjoyed visiting a member of your family in their home.

You should say:
who you visited and where they lived
why you made this visit
what happened during this visit

and explain what you enjoyed about this visit.

You will have to talk about the topic for one to two minutes. You have one minute to think about what you are going to say. You can make some notes to help you if you wish.

PART 3

Discussion topics:

Family occasions

Example questions:
When do families celebrate together in your country?
How often do all the generations in a family come together in your country?
Why is it that some people might *not* enjoy attending family occasions?

Everyday life in families

Example questions:
Do you think it is a good thing for parents to help their children with schoolwork?
How important do you think it is for families to eat together at least once a day?
Do you believe that everyone in a family should share household tasks?

Test 4

LISTENING

Listening test audio

PART 1 *Questions 1–10*

Complete the notes below.

*Write **ONE WORD AND/OR A NUMBER** for each answer.*

Job details from employment agency

Role **1** ....

Location Fordham **2** .... Centre

3 .... Road, Fordham

Work involves

- dealing with enquiries
- making **4** .... and reorganising them
- maintaining the internal **5** ....
- general administration

Requirements

- **6** .... (essential)
- a calm and **7** .... manner
- good IT skills

Other information

- a **8** .... job – further opportunities may be available
- hours: 7.45 a.m. to **9** .... p.m. Monday to Friday
- **10** .... is available onsite

→ p. 129 p. 118

PART 2 *Questions 11–20*

Listening test audio

Questions 11–14

Choose the correct letter, ***A****,* ***B*** *or* ***C****.*

11 The museum building was originally

A a factory.
B a private home.
C a hall of residence.

12 The university uses part of the museum building as

A teaching rooms.
B a research library.
C administration offices.

13 What does the guide say about the entrance fee?

A Visitors decide whether or not they wish to pay.
B Only children and students receive a discount.
C The museum charges extra for special exhibitions.

14 What are visitors advised to leave in the cloakroom?

A cameras
B coats
C bags

Questions 15–20

What information does the speaker give about each of the following areas of the museum?

*Choose **SIX** answers from the box and write the correct letter, **A–H**, next to Questions 15–20.*

Information

A Parents must supervise their children.
B There are new things to see.
C It is closed today.
D This is only for school groups.
E There is a quiz for visitors.
F It features something created by students.
G An expert is here today.
H There is a one-way system.

Areas of museum

15 Four Seasons ....
16 Farmhouse Kitchen ....
17 A Year on the Farm ....
18 Wagon Walk ....
19 Bees are Magic ....
20 The Pond ....

 → p. 129 p. 119

PART 3 *Questions 21–30*

Questions 21 and 22

*Choose **TWO** letters, **A–E**.*

Which **TWO** educational skills were shown in the video of children doing origami?

A solving problems
B following instructions
C working cooperatively
D learning through play
E developing hand–eye coordination

Questions 23–27

Which comment do the students make about each of the following children in the video?

*Choose **SIX** answers from the box and write the correct letter, **A–G**, next to Questions 23–27.*

Comments	
A	demonstrated independence
B	asked for teacher support
C	developed a competitive attitude
D	seemed to find the activity calming
E	seemed pleased with the results
F	seemed confused
G	seemed to find the activity easy

Children

23 Sid ....

24 Jack ....

25 Naomi ....

26 Anya ....

27 Zara ....

Questions 28–30

*Choose the correct letter, **A**, **B** or **C**.*

28 Before starting an origami activity in class, the students think it is important for the teacher to

A make models that demonstrate the different stages.
B check children understand the terminology involved.
C tell children not to worry if they find the activity difficult.

29 The students agree that some teachers might be unwilling to use origami in class because

A they may not think that crafts are important.
B they may not have the necessary skills.
C they may worry that it will take up too much time.

30 Why do the students decide to use origami in their maths teaching practice?

A to correct a particular misunderstanding
B to set a challenge
C to introduce a new concept

→ 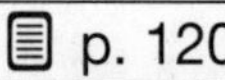 p. 129 p. 120

PART 4 Questions 31–40

Listening test audio

Complete the notes below.

*Write **ONE WORD ONLY** for each answer.*

Victor Hugo

His novel, *Les Misérables*

- It has been adapted for theatre and cinema.
- We know more about its overall **31** .... than about its author.

His early career

- In Paris, his career was successful and he led the Romantic movement.
- He spoke publicly about social issues, such as **32** .... and education.
- Napoleon III disliked his views and exiled him.

His exile from France

- Victor Hugo had to live elsewhere in **33** ....
- He used his income from the sale of some **34** .... he had written to buy a house on Guernsey.

His house on Guernsey

- Victor Hugo lived in this house until the end of the Empire in France.
- The ground floor contains portraits, **35** .... and tapestries that he valued.
- He bought cheap **36** .... made of wood and turned this into beautiful wall carvings.
- The first floor consists of furnished areas with wallpaper and **37** .... that have a Chinese design.
- The library still contains many of his favourite books.
- He wrote in a room at the top of the house that had a view of the **38** ....
- He entertained other writers as well as poor **39** .... in his house.
- Victor Hugo's **40** .... gave ownership of the house to the city of Paris in 1927.

→ p. 129 p. 121

READING

SECTION 1 *Questions 1–14*

Read the text below and answer Questions 1–7.

The best ice cream makers

Have you ever considered making ice cream at home but thought it would be too complicated? Here is a selection of machines that could change your mind

A Magimix Gelato Expert

If you're an ice cream fanatic, it doesn't get better than this. It's quick, taking as little as 20 minutes, and consistent in its results, while the three automated programmes are very easy to use and it has an unusually generous two-litre capacity. On the other hand, we found it noisier than many, and the ice cream is softer than we might have liked.

B Shake n Make Ice Cream Maker

If you want to make some basic soft ice cream, this is a fun little gadget that gets decent results. You add a little ice and salt to the base, then your ingredients to the stainless-steel tub, pop the lid on and give it a good shake for at least three minutes. Provided you measure everything exactly and shake back and forth consistently, it's surprisingly efficient.

C Sage Smart Scoop

This is a seriously smart machine. Our favourite feature is the built-in sensor that works out whether the consistency of your ice cream or frozen yoghurt is right for you (from the 12 hardness settings) so that it can stop mixing when it's ready, alerting you with a fun tune. As you'd expect from the considerable price tag, there's a built-in freezer and it feels beautifully engineered.

D Lakeland Digital Ice Cream Maker

You simply pop on the lid and pour in the ingredients, then set the timer using the nice, clear digital display. Some customers reportedly struggled to disassemble it in order to wash the bowl and paddle, but we didn't have that problem. We're also giving it extra points for the recipe book, which has some really tasty ideas.

E Judge Ice Cream Maker

We had a few criticisms, perhaps not surprisingly when you consider this is one of the cheapest models in our selection – notably the fact that the paddle isn't as robust as the ones in other models. We'd have liked more recipes, too. But, for a budget machine, this is a bargain.

F KitchenAid Artisan Ice Cream Maker

If you own a KitchenAid food mixer, this attachment (one of 15 that fits this machine) is a good way to start ice cream making. You simply freeze the bowl before use and attach it to the mixer (a quick and easy job) and pour in your favourite fresh ingredients, with some recipes taking just 20 minutes.

Questions 1–7

Look at the six advertisements for ice cream makers, **A–F**, on pages 86 and 87.

For which ice cream maker are the following statements true?

Write the correct letter, ***A–F****, in boxes 1–7 on your answer sheet.*

NB *You may use any letter more than once.*

1 Users of this machine will need to put some physical effort into making ice cream.

2 Users of this machine can decide how soft they want their ice cream to be.

3 This ice cream maker can be fixed onto an existing kitchen appliance.

4 It is possible to make a larger amount of ice cream at one time than in most other machines.

5 This machine has features that make it worth the high price.

6 People might find it difficult to take this machine apart.

7 This machine makes an enjoyable sound when the ice cream is prepared.

Read the text below and answer Questions 8–14.

Photography weekend course on the coast of Cornwall

Our three-night photography weekend is designed to appeal to all levels. Participants will be able to enjoy some of the fantastic locations on this beautiful coastline, with its ever-changing light, while staying in a comfortable hotel and enjoying some typical dishes of this south-western region of Britain.

Price includes: Personal daily tuition, discussions, welcome reception, and dinner, bed and breakfast for three nights in a twin or double room.

Price does not include: Insurance and photographic equipment plus transport to photographic venues. Participants are required to arrange this. Car share during the weekend is a popular option.

Course information

- Our courses are relaxed but comprehensive, and the content is largely dictated by those attending. Included within the sessions are editing workshops at the hotel and photo shoots down by the sea. Visits further away are also undertaken to experiment with different landscapes.

- Arrival by mid-afternoon on the first day will allow you to check into the hotel and enjoy some Cornish refreshments before heading out into the fresh air for our first shoot together at sunset. Dinner and a good night's sleep and you'll be ready to start at sunrise the next day. In the evenings you will have a chance to unwind at the hotel, share your thoughts on the day and spend time looking at images and sharing editing techniques.

- Maximum numbers: Four photographers per course.

- The following equipment is essential: A digital SLR or bridge camera with its instruction manual, batteries and charger; memory cards; comfortable walking footwear with good grip; warm outdoor clothing and waterproofs.

- Recommended equipment: A tripod, filters, a laptop with editing software and charger.

Questions 8–14

Do the following statements agree with the information given in the text on page 89?

In boxes 8–14 on your answer sheet, write

TRUE	*if the statement agrees with the information*
FALSE	*if the statement contradicts the information*
NOT GIVEN	*if there is no information on this*

8 The course is aimed at people who are already skilled photographers.

9 Three meals a day are included in the course fee.

10 The only way to reach the hotel is by car.

11 The topics covered on the course depend mainly on the wishes of the participants.

12 Participants are expected to get up early on their first morning to take photographs.

13 The tutor will show participants examples of her work after dinner.

14 Participants should be prepared for bad weather.

 → p. 130

SECTION 2 *Questions 15–27*

Read the text below and answer Questions 15–21.

Respiratory Protective Equipment – advice for factory employees

You need to wear Respiratory Protective Equipment (RPE) when you're doing work where you could breathe in hazardous substances in the air such as dust, vapour or gas. Common health effects from breathing hazardous substances include sore eyes and headaches. Make sure you are using the right RPE for the task. For example, negative pressure respirators should not be used in low oxygen environments.

Some types of RPE must have a tight seal around the facial area to be effective. Your employer will arrange a yearly facial fit test to ensure that you are given RPE that fits properly. This checks that the seal between the respirator and the facial area is secure, by releasing a substance that you can smell or taste if the RPE is not working properly. RPE will only provide effective protection if you are clean shaven. Facial hair growth makes it almost impossible to get a good seal so, if you have a beard, you should talk to your employer about other forms of RPE that do not rely on a tight facial fit. Jewellery and long hair can also compromise an effective fit.

Using your RPE

You should complete a visual check of your RPE for signs of damage before you use it. If you are using RPE that requires a tight fit, you must check it fits properly before entering a hazardous area.

Cleaning your RPE

Wash and dry your RPE after using it. Use a mild detergent, as harsh products such as solvents can cause damage. Use a brush and warm water and rinse with clean water. This will remove excess detergent that can cause skin irritation. Dry your RPE on a solid wooden rack or suspend from a clothes line.

Maintaining your RPE

Inspect your RPE after each use and during cleaning. Make sure you check the straps for breaks, tears, fraying edges and deterioration of elasticity. Check the inhalation and exhalation valves are working and not damaged.

Storing your RPE

Improper storage can cause distortion to your RPE. Store your RPE in a clean, dry place, away from dust, oil and sunlight. RPE should be stored so that it doesn't get crushed.

Questions 15–21

Complete the sentences below.

*Choose **ONE WORD** from the text for each answer.*

Write your answers in boxes 15–21 on your answer sheet.

15 Some respirators are unsuitable for use in areas with limited levels of ………………………… .

16 Facial fit tests should be conducted on a ………………………… basis.

17 For workers who have a ………………………… , an alternative to tight-fitting RPE may be required.

18 Workers should avoid cleaning their RPE with ………………………… .

19 RPE can either be hung up or placed on a timber ………………………… in order to dry it.

20 It is important to ensure that the RPE ………………………… are not ripped and can still stretch.

21 RPE should not be exposed to direct ………………………… when it is being stored.

Read the text below and answer Questions 22–27.

Working with cows in a dairy
Guidelines for employers

Slips and trips

Slips and trips are one of the most common accidents when working in farm dairies. They often happen when working with cows in a dairy during milking, and during maintenance and cleaning.

The following three hazards make it more likely that employees will slip or trip:

1. Surfaces which are wet or dirty
   - Have a system for cleaning up milk, oil, cleaning fluid and grain spills as soon as they happen, and make sure it is followed.
   - Install non-slip mats in wet work areas and make sure that footwear is slip-resistant.
2. Obstacles such as pipes or cables in the farm dairy
   - Reduce tripping accidents by hanging hoses and pipes along walls out of people's way and remove unused fittings, like bolt fasteners in floors.
   - Move obstacles from walkways and entrances where possible. Tripping hazards which cannot be removed should be clearly indicated with yellow tape. If there are obstacles overhead, these should be wrapped in padding to avoid risk of injury.
3. Steps which are too high or not deep enough, or steps in poorly lit areas
   - Build steps properly and use non-slip surfaces.
   - Handrails should also be fitted.
   - The provision of good lighting can also help to reduce the risk of injury.

Lifting and carrying

The following tasks pose risks to dairy workers:

- lifting buckets of grain, water and milk
- lifting calves.

Managing the hazards

- Balance the load by using two buckets, one in each hand.
- Where possible, use trolleys and other mechanical aids to replace manual tasks.

Milking by hand

Specific tasks in milking which cause injury are:

- bending in an awkward position
- putting on and removing milking equipment from cows.

Managing the hazards

- Think about designing or changing the milking area so workers can change the height they are working at to suit them. Ensure that all equipment needed is close by to avoid workers having to overreach or adopt a bending position.
- Alternate between jobs to reduce repetitious manual handling tasks, including a rotation between putting on and removing milking equipment.

Questions 22–27

Complete the table below.

*Choose **ONE WORD ONLY** from the text for each answer.*

Write your answers in boxes 22–27 on your answer sheet.

Hazard	Managing the hazard
Slips and trips	
Slippery floor surfaces	Remove solid spills such as grain immediately. Ensure all items of **22** .... have good grip.
Hoses and pipes	Ensure they are fitted to walls where possible. Highlight obstructions with brightly coloured tape.
Overhead obstacles	Ensure they are covered with **23** ....
Unsuitable steps	Provide good lighting and install **24** ....
Lifting and carrying	
Transporting containers and calves	Spread the weight evenly between both hands. Try to avoid moving containers by hand, and use equipment such as **25** .... instead.
Milking by hand	
Repetitive handling of milking equipment	Keep everything accessible so that employees don't need to bend or **26** .... Introduce a system of **27** .... to increase variety.

→ p. 130

SECTION 3 *Questions 28–40*

Read the text on pages 97 and 98 and answer Questions 28–40.

Questions 28–34

The text on pages 97 and 98 has seven sections, **A–G**.

Choose the correct heading for each section from the list of headings below.

Write the correct number, ***i–viii****, in boxes 28–34 on your answer sheet.*

List of Headings

- **i** How chance contributes to conditions being right
- **ii** Concern about the changing environment
- **iii** The process of photographing animals at night is getting easier
- **iv** How human developments are affecting wildlife
- **v** Photographing objects that can't be seen in detail
- **vi** A season that may seem unsuitable for photographers
- **vii** No longer too expensive
- **viii** A less ambitious approach

28 Section **A**

29 Section **B**

30 Section **C**

31 Section **D**

32 Section **E**

33 Section **F**

34 Section **G**

Night photography in autumn

A November in the northern hemisphere is not the most inspiring of months for the photographer. The days shorten appreciably as winter approaches and the last autumn leaves are blown free by high winds and frequent rain. Nature seems dormant, as many birds have long since flown to warmer climates, fungi break through the earth, and many animal species sleep until spring's warm awakening.

It would seem a good time also to put the camera to bed and forget about photography until the first snowfall. Well, not quite. With the days being shorter and daylight less bright, November is an excellent month to turn your attention to what can be found in the long darkness from dusk to dawn. In the nocturnal hours a vast number of life forms still thrive, and provide a completely different set of subjects to those the daylight hours present.

B As the most noticeable object in the night sky, the moon is an obvious subject when making your initial attempts at night photography. The timing of an evening moonrise is important to know because, not only does it vary according to the time of year, but the moon always appears largest at this point, when it is closest to the horizon. To capture the moon at its brilliant best, you need a bit of luck too: a time when its brightest phase – a full moon – coincides with the ideal weather forecast of a cloudless night sky. The moon is not a direct light source such as the sun or the stars; instead it is reflecting the light of the sun hitting its surface. On such a night, a full moon will reflect only about ten percent of the sunlight, but that is still enough to illuminate buildings, trees, bridges and other landscape features.

C With today's cameras, far greater detail can be rendered. Whole constellations consisting of thousands of points of starlight filling the frame and even galaxies such as our own Milky Way can be captured. This is a type of night photography for which few of us had suitable equipment a decade ago, but now it has become accessible to all photographers, thanks to the much improved, affordable technology.

However, photographers choosing to shoot the moon may be less concerned by this, as they tend to prefer to use telephoto lenses to magnify the size of the moon, particularly when it is low in the sky and can be shown in relation to a landmark or recognisable structure within the frame.

D Of course, the nocturnal world offers other subjects closer to the ground, some that are even familiar to us by day. As cities and towns spread further into our green spaces, some wild animals move further afield to escape our intrusions, while others adapt to their new urbanised surroundings.

In European cities, sightings of foxes at night are increasingly common, as they thrive thanks to the cover of darkness and a ready supply of residents' waste bins, which they use as feeding stations. Deer and wild boar are larger mammals that have also adapted to the urban fringes in recent years, emerging from the cover of parks and nearby forests to forage in residential gardens by night.

E Such is the proliferation of urban wildlife that some photographers now specialise in documenting the nocturnal animals that have developed a taste for city nightlife. The improvement in camera technology that has made night sky images more accessible has also extended the creative repertoire of the wildlife photographer. It is now possible to photograph some wild species at night, or soon after dusk, without having to always resort to the use of specialist equipment.

More exciting still is how the techniques of astro-photography and the wildlife camera-trap have combined in recent years, to produce images of nocturnal animals against a background of a star-studded night sky. This marriage of two photographic genres has created an innovative style of night photography.

F If that all sounds a bit too complex and time-consuming, with too many variables to spoil the hoped-for result, then consider using the fading light of the night sky in the brief time after dusk in a more opportunistic manner. Dusk is the part of the nocturnal phase when the light of the sun is still visible, though the sun itself has disappeared completely. During the earliest phase of dusk there is enough ambient light remaining to enable features in our surroundings to be seen without the aid of artificial light sources such as floodlights or street lamps.

G While many of us shoot sunsets, the period of dusk also provides an opportunity to use the ambient light low in the sky as a backdrop to photographing foreground subjects in varying stages of illumination, or even as shadowy outlines against the fading sky. The variety of possible subjects includes ships at sea, flocks of low-flying birds, trees, windmills, skyscrapers and high bridges. These are all well known by day, but against a night sky at dusk they lack colour, so any compositional strength is determined by the graphic appeal of their distinct and recognisable shapes.

Questions 35–40

Complete the sentences below.

Choose ***ONE WORD ONLY*** *from the text for each answer.*

Write your answers in boxes 35–40 on your answer sheet.

35 November is a time when .... grow.

36 The apparent size of the moon depends on its position in relation to the ....

37 Sunlight is reflected by the .... of the moon.

38 When the night sky is clear, many objects in the ...., e.g., buildings, are visible.

39 With modern cameras, it is possible to photograph not only constellations but also ....

40 Deer and wild boar may search for food in .... in towns.

→ p. 130

WRITING

WRITING TASK 1

You should spend about 20 minutes on this task.

You recently attended a training course for your work. Your employer has asked you for your feedback on the training course.

Write a letter to your employer. In your letter

- ***remind your employer what the course was about***
- ***explain why the course was useful to you in your work***
- ***suggest why the course may*** **not** ***be suitable for some of your other colleagues***

Write at least 150 words.

You do **NOT** need to write any addresses.

Begin your letter as follows:

Dear ....,

→ p. 138

WRITING TASK 2

You should spend about 40 minutes on this task.

Write about the following topic:

> ***Some people dislike changes in their society and in their own lives, and want things to stay the same.***
>
> ***Why do some people want things to stay the same?***
>
> ***Why should change be regarded as something positive?***

Give reasons for your answer and include any relevant examples from your own knowledge or experience.

Write at least 250 words.

→ p. 139

SPEAKING

PART 1

The examiner asks you about yourself, your home, work or studies and other familiar topics.

EXAMPLE

Sleep

- How many hours do you usually sleep at night?
- Do you sometimes sleep during the day? [Why/Why not?]
- What do you do if you can't get to sleep at night? [Why?]
- Do you ever remember the dreams you've had while you were asleep?

PART 2

Describe a time when you met someone who you became good friends with.

You should say:

who you met
when and where you met this person
what you thought about this person when you first met

and explain why you think you became good friends with this person.

You will have to talk about the topic for one to two minutes. You have one minute to think about what you are going to say. You can make some notes to help you if you wish.

PART 3

Discussion topics:

Friends at school

Example questions:
How important is it for children to have lots of friends at school?
Do you think it is wrong for parents to influence which friends their children have?
Why do you think children often choose different friends as they get older?

Making new friends

Example questions:
If a person is moving to a new town, what is a good way for them to make friends?
Can you think of any disadvantages of making new friends online?
Would you say it is harder for people to make new friends as they get older?

Audioscripts

TEST 1

PART 1

MAN: Excuse me. Would you mind if I asked you some questions? We're doing a survey on transport.
SADIE: Yes, that's OK.
MAN: First of all, can I take your name?
SADIE: Yes. It's Sadie Jones.
MAN: Thanks very much. And could I have your date of birth – just the year will do, actually. Is that all right?
SADIE: Yes, that's fine. It's 1991.
MAN: So next your postcode, please.
SADIE: It's DW30 7YZ. *Q1*
MAN: Great. Thanks. Is that in Wells?
SADIE: No it's actually in Harborne – Wells isn't far from there though.
MAN: I really like that area. My grandmother lived there when I was a kid.
SADIE: Yes, it is nice.
MAN: Right so now I want to ask you some questions about how you travelled here today. Did you use public transport?
SADIE: Yes. I came by bus.
MAN: OK. And that was today. It's the 24th of April, isn't it? *Q2*
SADIE: Isn't it the 25th? No, actually, you're right.
MAN: Ha ha. And what was the reason for your trip today? I can see you've got some shopping with you.
SADIE: Yes. I did some shopping but the main reason I came here was to go to the dentist. *Q3*
MAN: That's not much fun. Hope it was nothing serious.
SADIE: No, it was just a check-up. It's fine.
MAN: Good. Do you normally travel by bus into the city centre?
SADIE: Yes. I stopped driving in ages ago because parking was so difficult to find and it costs so much. *Q4*
MAN: I see.
SADIE: The bus is much more convenient too. It only takes about 30 minutes.
MAN: That's good. So where did you start your journey?
SADIE: At the bus stop on Claxby Street. *Q5*
MAN: Is that C-L-A–X-B-Y?
SADIE: That's right.

MAN: And how satisfied with the service are you? Do you have any complaints?
SADIE: Well, as I said, it's very convenient and quick when it's on time, but this morning it was late. Only about 10 minutes, but still. *Q6*
MAN: Yes, I understand that's annoying. And what about the timetable? Do you have any comments about that?
SADIE: Mmm. I suppose I mainly use the bus during the day, but any time I've been in town in the evening – for dinner or at the cinema – I've noticed you have to wait a long time for a bus – there aren't that many. *Q7*

MAN:	OK, thanks. So now I'd like to ask you about your car use.	
SADIE:	Well, I have got a car but I don't use it that often. Mainly just to go to the supermarket. But that's about it really. My husband uses it at the weekends to go to the golf club.	*Q8*
MAN:	And what about a bicycle?	
SADIE:	I don't actually have one at the moment.	
MAN:	What about the city bikes you can rent? Do you ever use those?	
SADIE:	No – I'm not keen on cycling there because of all the pollution. But I would like to get a bike – it would be good to use it to get to work.	*Q9*
MAN:	So why haven't you got one now?	
SADIE:	Well, I live in a flat – on the second floor and it doesn't have any storage – so we'd have to leave it in the hall outside the flat.	*Q10*
MAN:	I see. OK. Well, I think that's all ...	

PART 2

Good evening, everyone. Let me start by welcoming you all to this talk and thanking you for taking the time to consider joining ACE voluntary organisation. ACE offers support to people and services in the local area and we're now looking for more volunteers to help us do this.

By the way, I hope you're all comfortable – we have brought in extra seats so that no one has to stand, but it does mean that the people at the back of the room may be a bit squashed. We'll only be here for about half an hour so, hopefully, that's OK. *Q11*

One of the first questions we're often asked is how old you need to be to volunteer. Well, you can be as young as 16 or you can be 60 or over; it all depends on what type of voluntary work you want to do. Other considerations, such as reliability, are crucial in voluntary work and age isn't related to these, in our experience. *Q12*

Another question we get asked relates to training. Well, there's plenty of that and it's all face-to-face. What's more, training doesn't end when you start working for us – it takes place before, during and after periods of work. Often, it's run by other experienced volunteers as managers tend to prefer to get on with other things. *Q13*

Now, I would ask *you* to consider a couple of important issues before you decide to apply for voluntary work. We don't worry about why you want to be a volunteer – people have many different reasons that range from getting work experience to just doing something they've always wanted to do. But it is critical that you have enough hours in the day for whatever role we agree is suitable for you – if being a volunteer becomes stressful then it's best not to do it at all. You may think that your income is important, but we don't ask about that. It's up to you to decide if you can work without earning money. What we value is dedication. Some of our most loyal volunteers earn very little themselves but still give their full energy to the work they do with us. *Q14/15* *Q14/15*

OK, so let's take a look at some of the work areas that we need volunteers for and the sort of things that would help you in those.

You may wish simply to help us raise money. If you have the creativity to come up with an imaginative or novel way of fundraising, we'd be delighted, as standing in the local streets or shops with a collection box can be rather boring! *Q16*

One outdoor activity that we need volunteers for is litter collection and for this it's useful if you can walk for long periods, sometimes uphill. Some of our regular collectors are quite elderly, but very active and keen to protect the environment. *Q17*

If you enjoy working with children, we have three vacancies for what are called 'playmates'. These volunteers help children learn about staying healthy through a range of out-of-school activities. You don't need to have children yourself, but it's good if you know something about nutrition and can give clear instructions. Q18

If that doesn't appeal to you, maybe you would be interested in helping out at our story club for disabled children, especially if you have done some acting. We put on three performances a year based on books they have read and we're always looking for support with the theatrical side of this. Q19

The last area I'll mention today is first aid. Volunteers who join this group can end up teaching others in vulnerable groups who may be at risk of injury. Initially, though, your priority will be to take in a lot of information and not forget any important steps or details. Q20

Right, so does anyone have any questions …

PART 3

HUGO: Hi Chantal. What did you think of the talk, then?
CHANTAL: Hi Hugo. I thought it was good once I'd moved seats.
HUGO: Oh – were the people beside you chatting or something?
CHANTAL: It wasn't that. I went early so that I'd get a seat and not have to stand, but then this guy sat right in front of me and he was so tall! Q21
HUGO: It's hard to see through people's heads, isn't it?
CHANTAL: Impossible! Anyway, to answer your question, I thought it was really interesting, especially what the speaker said about the job market.
HUGO: Me too. I mean we know we're going into a really competitive field so it's obvious that we may struggle to get work.
CHANTAL: That's right – and we know we can't all have that 'dream job'.
HUGO: Yeah, but it looks like there's a whole range of … areas of work that we hadn't even thought of – like fashion journalism, for instance. Q22
CHANTAL: Yeah – I wasn't expecting so many career options.
HUGO: Mmm. Overall, she had quite a strong message, didn't she?
CHANTAL: She did. She kept saying things like 'I know you all think this, but …' and then she'd tell us how it really is.
HUGO: Perhaps she thinks students are a bit narrow-minded about the industry.
CHANTAL: It was a bit harsh, though! We know it's a tough industry. Q23
HUGO: Yeah – and we're only first years, after all. We've got a lot to learn.
CHANTAL: Exactly. Do you think our secondary-school education should have been more career-focused?
HUGO: Well, we had numerous talks on careers, which was good, but none of them were very inspiring. They could have asked more people like today's speaker to talk to us. Q24
CHANTAL: I agree. We were told about lots of different careers – just when we needed to be, but not by the experts who really know stuff.
HUGO: So did today's talk influence your thoughts on what career you'd like to take up in the future?
CHANTAL: Well, I promised myself that I'd go through this course and keep an open mind till the end. Q25
HUGO: But I think it's better to pick an area of the industry now and then aim to get better and better at it.

CHANTAL: Well, I think we'll just have to differ on that issue!
HUGO: One thing's for certain, though. From what she said, we'll be unpaid assistants in the industry for quite a long time.
CHANTAL: Mmm.
HUGO: I'm prepared for that, aren't you? *Q26*
CHANTAL: Actually, I'm not going to accept that view.
HUGO: Really? But she *knows* it's the case – and everyone else says the same.
CHANTAL: That doesn't mean it has to be true for me.
HUGO: OK. Well – I hope you're right!

CHANTAL: I thought the speaker's account of her first job was fascinating.
HUGO: Yeah – she admitted she was lucky to get work being a personal dresser for a musician. She didn't even apply for the job and there she was getting paid to choose all his clothes.
CHANTAL: It must have felt amazing – though she said all she was looking for back then was experience, not financial reward.
HUGO: Mmm. And then he was so mean, telling her she was more interested in her own appearance than his! *Q27/28*
CHANTAL: But – she did realise he was right about that, which really made me think. I'm always considering my own clothes but now I can see you should be focusing on your client!
HUGO: She obviously regretted losing the job.
CHANTAL: Well, as she said, she should have hidden her negative feelings about him, but she didn't. *Q27/28*
HUGO: It was really brave the way she picked herself up and took that job in retail. Fancy working in a shop after that!
CHANTAL: Yeah – well, she recommended we all do it at some point. I guess as a designer you'd get to find out some useful information, like how big or small the average shopper is.
HUGO: I think that's an issue for manufacturers, not designers. However, it *would* be useful to know if there's a gap in the market – you know, an item that no one's stocking but that consumers are looking for. *Q29/30*
CHANTAL: Yeah, people don't give up searching. They also take things back to the store if they aren't right.
HUGO: Yeah. Imagine you worked in an expensive shop and you found out the garments sold there were being returned because they … fell apart in the wash! *Q29/30*
CHANTAL: Yeah, it would be good to know that kind of thing.
HUGO: Yeah.

PART 4

For my presentation today I want to tell you about how groups of elephants have been moved and settled in new reserves. This is known as translocation and has been carried out in Malawi in Africa in recent years. The reason this is being done is because of overpopulation of elephants in some areas.

Overpopulation is a good problem to have and not one we tend to hear about very often. In Malawi's Majete National Park the elephant population had been wiped out by poachers, who killed the elephants for their ivory. But in 2003, the park was restocked and effective law enforcement was introduced. Since then, not a single elephant has been poached. In this safe environment, the elephant population boomed. Breeding went so well that there were more elephants than the park could support.

This led to a number of problems. Firstly, there was more competition for food, which meant that some elephants were suffering from hunger. As there was a limit to the amount of food in the national park, some elephants began looking further afield. Elephants were routinely knocking down fences around the park, which then had to be repaired at a significant cost. Q31

To solve this problem, the decision was made to move dozens of elephants from Majete National Park to Nkhotakota Wildlife Park, where there were no elephants. But, obviously, attempting to move significant numbers of elephants to a new home 300 kilometres away is quite a challenge.

So how did this translocation process work in practice?

Elephants were moved in groups of between eight and twenty, all belonging to one family. Q32 Because relationships are very important to elephants, they all had to be moved at the same time. A team of vets and park rangers flew over the park in helicopters and targeted a group, Q33 which were rounded up and directed to a designated open plain.

The vets then used darts to immobilise the elephants – this was a tricky manoeuvre, as they not only had to select the right dose of tranquiliser for different-sized elephants but they had to dart the elephants as they were running around. This also had to be done as quickly as Q34 possible so as to minimise the stress caused. As soon as the elephants began to flop onto the ground, the team moved in to take care of them.

To avoid the risk of suffocation, the team had to make sure none of the elephants were lying Q35 on their chests because their lungs could be crushed in this position. So all the elephants had to be placed on their sides. One person stayed with each elephant while they waited for the vets to do checks. It was very important to keep an eye on their breathing – if there were Q36 fewer than six breaths per minute, the elephant would need urgent medical attention. Collars were fitted to the matriarch in each group so their movements could be tracked in their new home. Measurements were taken of each elephant's tusks – elephants with large tusks would Q37 be at greater risk from poachers – and also of their feet. The elephants were then taken to a recovery area before being loaded onto trucks and transported to their new home.

The elephants translocated to Nkhotakota settled in very well and the project has generally been accepted to have been a huge success – and not just for the elephants. Employment Q38 prospects have improved enormously, contributing to rising living standards for the whole community. Poaching is no longer an issue, as former poachers are able to find more reliable sources of income. In fact, many of them volunteered to give up their weapons, as they were Q39 no longer of any use to them.

More than two dozen elephants have been born at Nkhotakota since relocation. With an area of more than 1,800 square kilometres, there's plenty of space for the elephant population to continue to grow. Their presence is also helping to rebalance Nkhotakota's damaged ecosystem and providing a sustainable conservation model, which could be replicated in other parks. All this has been a big draw for tourism, which contributes five times more than Q40 the illegal wildlife trade to GDP, and this is mainly because of the elephants. There's also been a dramatic rise in interest …

TEST 2

PART 1

WOMAN: So, I understand you're interested in restaurant work?

MAN: Yes. I've got a bit of experience and I can provide references.

WOMAN: That's good. I can check all that later. Now, Milo's Restaurants have some vacancies at the moment. They're a really good company to work for. Lots of benefits.

MAN: Oh right.

WOMAN: Yes. They've got a very good reputation for looking after staff. For example, all employees get training – even temporary staff. *Q1*

MAN: Oh really? That's quite unusual, isn't it?

WOMAN: Certainly is.

MAN: And do staff get free uniforms too?

WOMAN: Um … you just need to wear a white T-shirt and black trousers, it says here. So I guess not … But another benefit of working for a big company like this is that you can get a discount at any of their restaurants. *Q2*

MAN: Even at weekends?

WOMAN: No, but you'll be working then anyway.

MAN: Oh yes. I suppose so. Most of their restaurants are in the city centre, aren't they? So, easy to get to by bus?

WOMAN: Yes. That's right. But if you have to do a late shift and finish work after midnight, *Q3*
the company will pay for you to get a taxi home.

MAN: I probably won't need one. I think I'd use my bike.

WOMAN: OK. Now, they do have some quite specific requirements for the kind of person they're looking for. Milo's is a young, dynamic company and they're really keen on creating a strong team. It's really important that you can fit in and get on well with everyone.

MAN: Yeah. I've got no problem with that. It sounds good, actually. The last place I worked for was quite demanding too. We had to make sure we gave a really high *Q4*
level of service.

WOMAN: That's good to hear because that will be equally important at Milo's. I know they want people who have an eye for detail.

MAN: That's fine. I'm very used to working in that kind of environment.

WOMAN: Perfect. So the only other thing that's required is good communication skills, so you'll need to have a certificate in English. *Q5*

MAN: Sure.

WOMAN: OK. Let's have a look at the current job vacancies at Milo's. The first one is in Wivenhoe Street. *Q6*

MAN: Sorry, where?

WOMAN: Wivenhoe. W-I-V-E-N-H-O-E. It's quite central, just off Cork Street.

MAN: Oh right.

WOMAN: They're looking for a breakfast supervisor.

MAN: That would be OK.

WOMAN: So you're probably familiar with the kind of responsibilities involved. Obviously checking that all the portions are correct, etc., and then things like checking all *Q7*
the procedures for cleaning the equipment are being followed.

MAN: OK. And what about the salary? In my last job I was getting £9.50 per hour. I was hoping to get a bit more than that.

WOMAN: Well, to begin with, you'd be getting £9.75 but that goes up to £11.25 after three months. *Q8*

MAN: That's not too bad. And I suppose it's a very early start?

WOMAN: Mmm. That's the only unattractive thing about this job. But then you have the afternoons and evenings free. So the restaurant starts serving breakfast from 7 a.m. And you'd have to be there at 5.30 to set everything up. But you'd be finished at 12.30.

MAN: Mmm. Well, as you say, there are advantages to that.

WOMAN: Now, you might also be interested in the job at the City Road branch. That's for a junior chef, so again a position of responsibility.

MAN: I might prefer that, actually.

WOMAN: Right, well obviously this role would involve supporting the sous chef and other senior staff. And you'd be responsible for making sure there's enough stock each week – and sorting out all the deliveries. *Q9*

MAN: I've never done that before, but I imagine it's fairly straightforward, once you get the hang of it.

WOMAN: Yes, and you'd be working alongside more experienced staff to begin with, so I'm sure it wouldn't be a problem. The salary's slightly higher here. It's an annual salary of £23,000.

MAN: Right.

WOMAN: I know that if they like you, it's likely you'll be promoted quite quickly. So that's worth thinking about.

MAN: Yes. It does sound interesting. What are the hours like?

WOMAN: The usual, I think. There's a lot of evening and weekend work, but they're closed on Mondays. But you do get one Sunday off every four weeks. So would you like me to send off your … *Q10*

PART 2

Hello everyone. It's good to see that so many members of the public have shown up for our presentation on the new housing development planned on the outskirts of Nunston. I'm Mark Reynolds and I'm Communications Manager at the development.

I'll start by giving you a brief overview of our plans for the development. So one thing I'm sure you'll want to know is why we've selected this particular site for a housing development. At present it's being used for farming, like much of the land around Nunston. But because of the new industrial centre in Nunston, there's a lot of demand for housing for employees in the region, as many employees are having to commute long distances at present. Of course, there's also the fact that we have an international airport just 20 minutes' drive away, but although that's certainly convenient, it wasn't one of our major criteria for choosing the site. We were more interested in the fact that there's an excellent hospital just 15 kilometres away, and a large secondary school even closer than that. One drawback to the site is that it's on quite a steep slope, but we've taken account of that in our planning so it shouldn't be a major problem. *Q11/12* *Q11/12*

We've had a lot of positive feedback about the plans. People like the wide variety of accommodation types and prices, and the fact that it's only a short drive to get out into the countryside from the development. We were particularly pleased that so many people liked the designs for the layout of the development, with the majority of people saying it generally made a good impression and blended in well with the natural features of the landscape, with provision made for protecting trees and wildlife on the site. Some people have mentioned that they'd like to see more facilities for cyclists, and we'll look at that, but the overall feedback has been that the design and facilities of the development make it seem a place where people of all ages can live together happily. *Q13/14* *Q13/14*

OK. So I'll put a map of the proposed development up on the screen. You'll see it's bounded on the south side by the main road, which then goes on to Nunston. Another boundary is formed by London Road, on the western side of the development. Inside the development there'll be about 400 houses and 3 apartment blocks.

There'll also be a school for children up to 11 years old. If you look at the South Entrance at the bottom of the map, there's a road from there that goes right up through the development. The school will be on that road, at the corner of the second turning to the left. *Q15*

A large sports centre is planned with facilities for indoor and outdoor activities. This will be on the western side of the development, just below the road that branches off from London Road. *Q16*

There'll be a clinic where residents can go if they have any health problems. Can you see the lake towards the top of the map? The clinic will be just below this, to the right of a street of houses. *Q17*

There'll also be a community centre for people of all ages. On the northeast side of the development, there'll be a row of specially designed houses specifically for residents over 65, and the community centre will be adjoining this. *Q18*

We haven't forgotten about shopping. There'll be a supermarket between the two entrances to the development. We're planning to leave the three large trees near London Road, and it'll be just to the south of these. *Q19*

It's planned to have a playground for younger children. If you look at the road that goes up from the South Entrance, you'll see it curves round to the left at the top, and the playground will be in that curve, with nice views of the lake. *Q20*

OK, so now does anyone …

PART 3

ADAM: So, Michelle, shall we make a start on our presentation? We haven't got that much time left.

MICHELLE: No, Adam. But at least we've done all the background reading. I found it really interesting – I'd never even heard of the Laki eruption before this.

ADAM: Me neither. I suppose 1783 is a long time ago.

MICHELLE: But it was a huge eruption and it had such devastating consequences.

ADAM: I know. It was great there were so many primary sources to look at. It really gives you a sense of how catastrophic the volcano was. People were really trying to make sense of the science for the first time.

MICHELLE: That's right. But what I found more significant was how it impacted directly and indirectly on political events, as well as having massive social and economic consequences. *Q21*

ADAM: I know. That should be the main focus of our presentation.

MICHELLE: The observations made by people at the time were interesting, weren't they? I mean, they all gave a pretty consistent account of what happened, even if they didn't always use the same terminology.

ADAM: Yeah. I was surprised there were so many weather stations established by that time – so, you know, you can see how the weather changed, often by the hour. Q22

MICHELLE: Right. Writers at the time talked about the Laki haze to describe the volcanic fog that spread across Europe. They all realised that this wasn't the sort of fog they were used to – and of course this was in pre-industrial times – so they hadn't experienced sulphur-smelling fog before.

ADAM: No, that's true.

MICHELLE: Reports from the period blamed the haze for an increase in headaches, respiratory issues and asthma attacks. And they all describe how it covered the sun and made it look a strange red colour. Q23

ADAM: Must have been very weird.

MICHELLE: It's interesting that Benjamin Franklin wrote about the haze. Did you read that? He was the American ambassador in Paris at the time.

ADAM: Yeah. At first no one realised that the haze was caused by the volcanic eruption in Iceland.

MICHELLE: It was Benjamin Franklin who realised that before anyone else. Q24

ADAM: He's often credited with that, apparently. But a French naturalist beat him to it – I can't remember his name. I'd have to look it up. Then other naturalists had the same idea – all independently of each other.

MICHELLE: Oh right. We should talk about the immediate impact of the eruption, which was obviously enormous – especially in Iceland, where so many people died.

ADAM: Mmm. You'd expect that – and the fact that the volcanic ash drifted so swiftly – but not that the effects would go on for so long. Or that two years after the eruption, strange weather events were being reported as far away as North America and North Africa. Q25/26 Q25/26

MICHELLE: No. I found all that hard to believe too. It must have been terrible – and there was nothing anyone could do about it, even if they knew the ash cloud was coming in their direction.

MICHELLE: We should run through some of the terrible consequences of the eruption experienced in different countries. There's quite a varied range.

ADAM: Starting with Iceland, where the impact on farming was devastating.

MICHELLE: Mmm. One of the most dramatic things there was the effect on livestock as they grazed in the fields. They were poisoned because they ate vegetation that had been contaminated with fluorine as a result of the volcanic fallout. Q27

ADAM: That was horrible. In Egypt, the bizarre weather patterns led to a severe drought and as a result the Nile didn't flood, which meant the crops all failed.

MICHELLE: It's so far from where the eruption happened and yet the famine there led to more people dying than any other country. It was worse than the plague. Q28

ADAM: OK. Then in the UK the mortality rate went up a lot – presumably from respiratory illnesses. According to one report it was about double the usual number and included an unusually high percentage of people under the age of 25. Q29

MICHELLE: Mmm. I think people will be surprised to hear that the weather in the USA was badly affected too. George Washington even makes a note in his diary that they were snowbound until March in Virginia. That was before he became president.

ADAM: Yes, and there was ice floating down the Mississippi, which was unprecedented. Q30

MICHELLE: Astonishing, really. Anyway, what do you think …

PART 4

Good morning. Now, we've been asked to choose an aspect of European clothing or fashion and to talk about its development over time.

I decided to focus on a rather small area of clothing and that's pockets. I chose pockets for
two reasons, really. We all have them – in jeans, jackets, coats, for example – and even
though we often carry bags or briefcases as well, nothing is quite as convenient as being able *Q31*
to pop your phone or credit card into your pocket. Yet, I suspect that, other than that, people
don't really think about pockets too much and they're rather overlooked as a fashion item.

It's certainly very interesting to go back in time and see how pockets developed for men and
women. In the 18th century, fashions were quite different from the way they are now, and *Q32*
pockets were too. If we think about male fashion first … that was the time when suits became
popular. Trousers were knee-length only and referred to as 'breeches', the waistcoats were
short and the jackets were long, but all three garments were lined with material and pockets *Q33*
were sewn into this cloth by whichever tailor the customer used. The wearer could then carry
small objects such as pencils or coins on their person and reach them through a gap in the
lining. Coat pockets became increasingly decorative on the outside for men who wanted
to look stylish, but they were often larger but plainer if the wearer was someone with a *Q34*
profession who needed to carry medical instruments – a doctor or physician, for example.

The development of women's pockets was a little different. For one thing, they weren't nearly *Q35*
as visible or as easy to reach as men's. In the 18th and 19th centuries, women carried
numerous possessions on their person and some of these could be worth a lot of money.
Women were more vulnerable to theft and wealthy women, in particular, worried constantly
about pickpockets. So – what they did was to have a pair of pockets made that were tied *Q36*
together with string. The pockets were made of fabric, which might be recycled cloth if the
wearer had little money or something more expensive, such as linen, sometimes featuring
very delicate embroidery. Women tied the pockets around their waist so that they hung *Q37*
beneath their clothes. Remember, skirts were long then and there was plenty of room to hide
a whole range of small possessions between the layers of petticoats that were commonly
worn. They would have an opening in the folds of their skirts through which they could reach *Q38*
whatever they needed, like their perfume. Working women, of course, also needed to carry
around items that they might use for whatever job or trade they were involved in, but their
pairs of pockets still remained on the inside of their clothing, they just got bigger or longer –
sometimes reaching down to their knees!

So the tie-on pockets went well into the 19th century and only changed when fashion altered
towards the end of that period. That's when dresses became tighter and less bulky, and *Q39*
the pairs of pockets became very noticeable – they stood out too much and detracted from
the woman's image. Women who had been used to carrying around a range of personal
possessions – and still wanted to – needed somewhere to carry these items about their
person. That was when small bags, or pouches as they were known, came into fashion and,
of course, they inevitably led on to the handbag of more modern times, particularly when *Q40*
fashion removed pockets altogether.

TEST 3

PART 1

BREDA: Hello, Wayside Camera Club, Breda speaking.
DAN: Oh, hello, um, my name's Dan and I'd like to join your club.
BREDA: That's great, Dan. We have an application form – would you like to complete it over the phone, then you can ask any questions you might have?
DAN: Oh, yes, thanks.
BREDA: OK, so what's your family name?
DAN: It's Green – Dan Green.
BREDA: So – can I take your email address?
DAN: Yes, it's dan1068@market.com.
BREDA: Thanks. And what about your home address?
DAN: Well, I'm about ten miles away from your club in Peacetown. I live in a house there.
BREDA: OK, so what's the house number and street?
DAN: It's 52 Marrowfield Street. *Q1*
BREDA: Is that M-A double R-O-W-F-I-E-L-D?
DAN: That's right.
BREDA: … and that's Peacetown, you said?
DAN: Uhuh.

BREDA: So how did you hear about our club? Did you look on the internet?
DAN: I usually do that, but this time, well, I was talking to a relative the other day and he suggested it. *Q2*
BREDA: Oh, is he a member too?
DAN: He belongs to another club – but he'd heard good things about yours.
BREDA: OK. So what do you hope to get from joining?
DAN: Well, one thing that really interests me is the competitions that you have. I enjoy entering those.
BREDA: Right. Anything else?
DAN: Well, I also like to socialise with other photographers. *Q3*
BREDA: That's great. So what type of membership would you like?
DAN: What are the options?
BREDA: It's £30 a year for full membership or £20 a year if you're an associate. *Q4*
DAN: I think I'll go for the full membership, then.
BREDA: That's a good idea because you can't vote in meetings with an associate membership.

BREDA: If I could just find out a bit more about you …
DAN: OK.
BREDA: So you said you wanted to compete – have you ever won any photography competitions?
DAN: Not yet, but I have entered three in the past.
BREDA: Oh, that's interesting. So why don't you tell me something about those? Let's start with the first one.
DAN: Well, the theme was entitled 'Domestic Life'. *Q5*
BREDA: I see – so it had to be something related to the home?

DAN:	Yeah. I chose to take a photo of a family sitting round the dinner table having a meal, and, um, I didn't win, but I did get some feedback.	
BREDA:	Oh, what did the judges say?	
DAN:	That it was too 'busy' as a picture.	
BREDA:	Aha – so it was the composition of the picture that they criticised?	
DAN:	That's right – and once they'd told me that, I could see my mistake.	
BREDA:	So what was the theme of the second competition?	
DAN:	Well, my university was on the coast and that area gets a lot of beautiful sunsets, so that was the theme.	
BREDA:	Oh, sunsets, that's a great theme.	
DAN:	Yes. The instructions were to capture the clouds as well – it couldn't just be blue sky and a setting sun.	*Q6*
BREDA:	Sure, cause they give you all those amazing pinks and purples.	
DAN:	Yeah – and I thought I'd done that well, but the feedback was that I should have waited a bit longer to get the shot.	
BREDA:	I see. So the timing wasn't right.	*Q7*
DAN:	Yes – I took it too soon, basically. And then the third competition I entered was called 'Animal Magic'.	*Q8*
BREDA:	Well, that's a difficult subject!	
DAN:	I know! I had to take hundreds of shots.	
BREDA:	I'm sure – because animals move all the time.	
DAN:	That's what we had to show – there had to be some movement in the scene. I got a great shot of a fox in the end, but I took it at night and, well, I suspected that it was a bit dark, which is what I was told.	*Q9* *Q10*
BREDA:	Well Dan – you seem to be really keen and we'd be delighted to have you in our club. I'm sure we can help with all those areas that you've outlined.	
DAN:	Thanks, that's great.	

PART 2

PRESENTER:	This evening we're delighted to welcome Dan Beagle, who's just written a book on looking for and finding food in the wild. He's going to tell us everything we need to know about picking wild mushrooms.	
DAN:	Thank you very much. Well, I need to start by talking about safety. You really need to know what you're doing because some mushrooms are extremely poisonous. Having said that, once you know what to look for, it's really worth doing for the amazing variety of mushrooms available – which you can't get in the shops. But of course, you have to be very careful and that's why I always say you should never consume mushrooms picked by friends or neighbours – always remember that some poisonous mushrooms look very similar to edible ones and it's easy for people to get confused. The other thing to avoid is mushrooms growing beside busy roads for obvious reasons. But nothing beats the taste of freshly picked mushrooms – don't forget that the ones in the shops are often several days old and past their best.	*Q11/12* *Q11/12*
	There are certain ideas about wild mushrooms that it's important to be aware of. Don't listen to people who tell you that it's only OK to eat mushrooms that are pale or dull – this is completely untrue. Some edible mushrooms are bright red, for example. Personally, I prefer mushrooms cooked but it won't do you any harm to eat them uncooked in salads – it's not necessary to peel them. Another	*Q13/14*

thing you should remember is that you can't tell if a mushroom is safe to eat by its smell – some of the most deadly mushrooms have no smell and taste quite nice, apparently. Finally, just because deer or squirrels eat a particular mushroom doesn't mean that you can. Q13/14

Of course, mushroom picking is associated with the countryside but if you haven't got a car, your local park can be a great place to start. There are usually a range of habitats where mushrooms grow, such as playing fields and wooded areas. But you need to be there first thing in the morning, as there's likely be a lot of competition – not just from people but wildlife too. The deer often get the best mushrooms in my local park. Q15

If you're a complete beginner, I wouldn't recommend going alone or relying on photos in a book, even the one I've written! There are some really good phone apps for identifying mushrooms, but you can't always rely on getting a good signal in the middle of a wood. If possible, you should go with a group led by an expert – you'll stay safe and learn a lot that way. Q16

Conservation is a really important consideration and you must follow a few basic rules. You should never pick all the mushrooms in one area – collect only enough for your own needs. Be very careful that you don't trample on young mushrooms or other plants. And make sure you don't pick any mushrooms that are endangered and protected by law. Q17

There's been a decline in some varieties of wild mushrooms in this part of the country. Restaurants are becoming more interested in locally sourced food like wild mushrooms, but the biggest problem is that so many new houses have been built in this area in the last ten years. And more water is being taken from rivers and reservoirs because of this, and mushroom habitats have been destroyed. Q18

Anyway, a word of advice on storing mushrooms. Collect them in a brown paper bag and as soon as you get home, put them in the fridge. They'll be fine for a couple of days, but it's best to cook them as soon as possible – after washing them really carefully first, of course. Q19

So everybody knows what a mushroom tastes like, right? Well, you'll be surprised by the huge variety of wild mushrooms there are. Be adventurous! They're great in so many dishes – stir fries, risottos, pasta. But just be aware that some people can react badly to certain varieties so it's a good idea not to eat huge quantities to begin with. Q20

OK, so now I'm going to show you …

PART 3

YOUNG MAN: That seminar yesterday on automation and the future of work was really good, wasn't it? Looking at the first industrial revolution in Britain in the 19th century and seeing how people reacted to massive change was a real eye-opener.

YOUNG WOMAN: Yes. It was interesting to hear how people felt about automation then and what challenges they faced. I didn't know that first started with workers in the textile industry.

YOUNG MAN: With those protesting workers called the Luddites destroying their knitting machines because they were so worried about losing their jobs.

YOUNG WOMAN: Yes, and ultimately, they didn't achieve anything. And anyway, industrialisation created more jobs than it destroyed. *Q21/22*

YOUNG MAN: Yes, that's true – but it probably didn't seem a positive thing at the time. I can see why the Luddites felt so threatened. *Q21/22*

YOUNG WOMAN: I know. I'm sure I would have felt the same. The discussion about the future of work was really optimistic for a change. I like the idea that work won't involve doing boring, repetitive tasks, as robots will do all that. Normally, you only hear negative stuff about the future.

YOUNG MAN: Bit too optimistic, don't you think? For example, I can't see how people are about to have more leisure time, when all the evidence shows people are spending longer than ever at work. *Q23/24*

YOUNG WOMAN: No – that's true. And what about lower unemployment? I'm not so sure about that. *Q23/24*

YOUNG MAN: Perhaps in the long term – but not in the foreseeable future.

YOUNG WOMAN: Mmm. And I expect most people will be expected to work until they're much older – as everyone's living much longer.

YOUNG MAN: That's already happening.

YOUNG WOMAN: I enjoyed all that stuff on how technology has changed some jobs and how they're likely to change in the near future.

YOUNG MAN: Yeah, incredible. Like accountants. You might think all the technological innovations would have put them out of a job, but in fact there are more of them than ever. They're still really in demand and have become far more efficient. *Q25*

YOUNG WOMAN: Right. That was amazing. Twenty times more accountants in this country compared to the 19th century.

YOUNG MAN: I know. I'd never have thought that demand for hairdressing would have gone up so much in the last hundred years. One hairdresser for every 287 people now, compared to one for over 1,500.

YOUNG WOMAN: Yeah because people's earning power has gone up so they can afford to spend more on personal services like that. *Q26*

YOUNG MAN: But technology hasn't changed the actual job that much.

YOUNG WOMAN: No, they've got hairdryers, etc. but it's one job where you don't depend on a computer … The kind of work that administrative staff do has changed enormously, thanks to technology. Even 20 years ago there were secretaries doing dictation and typing.

YOUNG MAN: Yes. Really boring compared to these days, when they're given much more responsibility and higher status. *Q27*

YOUNG WOMAN: Mmm. A lot of graduates go in for this kind of work now … I'd expected there to be a much bigger change in the number of agricultural workers in the 19th century. But the 1871 census showed that roughly 25% of the population worked on the land.

YOUNG MAN: Yeah, I'd have assumed it would be more than 50%. Now it's less than 0.2%. *Q28*

YOUNG WOMAN: What about care workers?

YOUNG MAN: They barely existed in the 19th century as people's lifespan was so much shorter. But now of course this sector will see huge growth. *Q29*

YOUNG WOMAN: Yeah – and it's hard enough to meet current demand. The future looks quite bleak for bank clerks. They've been in decline since ATMs were introduced in the eighties.

YOUNG MAN: And technology will certainly make most of the jobs they do now redundant, I think. *Q30*

YOUNG WOMAN: I agree, although the situation may change. It's very hard to predict what will happen.

PART 4

In today's astronomy lecture, I'm going to talk about the need for a system to manage the movement of satellites and other objects in orbit around the Earth. In other words, a Space Traffic Management system. We already have effective Air Traffic Control systems that are used internationally to ensure that planes navigate our skies safely. Well, Space Traffic Management is a similar concept, but focusing on the control of satellites.

The aim of such a system would be to prevent the danger of collisions in space between the objects in orbit around the Earth. In order to do this, we'd need to have a set of legal measures, Q31
and we'd also have to develop the technical systems to enable us to prevent such accidents.

But unfortunately, at present we don't actually have a Space Traffic Management system that works. So why not? What are the problems in developing such a system?

Well, for one thing, satellites are relatively cheap these days, compared with how they were in the Q32
past, meaning that more people can afford to put them into space. So there's a lot more of them
out there, and people aren't just launching single satellites but whole constellations, consisting of Q33
thousands of them designed to work together. So space is getting more crowded every day.

But in spite of this, one thing you may be surprised to learn is that you can launch a satellite
into space and, once it's out there, it doesn't have to send back any information to Earth to Q34
allow its identification. So while we have international systems for ensuring we know where the *planes* in our skies are, and to prevent them from colliding with one another, when it
comes to the safety of *satellites*, at present we don't have anything like enough proper ways Q35
of tracking them.

And it isn't just entire satellites that we need to consider. A greater threat is the huge amount of space debris in orbit around the Earth – broken bits of satellite and junk from space stations and so on. And some of these are so small that they can be very hard to identify, but they can still be very dangerous.

In addition, some operators may be unwilling to share information about the satellites they've Q36
launched. For example, a satellite may be designed for military purposes, or it may have been launched for commercial reasons, and the operators don't want competitors to have information about it.

And even if the operators *are* willing to provide it, the information isn't easy to collect. Details are Q37
needed about the object itself, as well as about its location at a particular time – and remember that a satellite isn't very big, and it's likely to be moving at thousands of kilometres an hour.
We don't have any sensors that can constantly follow something moving so fast, so all that the Q38
scientists can do is to put forward a prediction concerning where the satellite is heading next.

So those are some of the problems that we're facing. Let's consider now some of the solutions that have been suggested. One key issue is the way in which information is dealt with. We need more information, but it also needs to be accessible at a global level, so we need to establish shared standards that we can all agree on for the way in which this information is presented. We already do this in other areas of science, so although this is a challenge, it's not an impossible task. Then, as all this information's collected, it needs to be put together so
it can be used, and that will involve creating a single database on which it can be entered. Q39

As we continue to push forward new developments, congestion of the space environment is only going to increase. To cope with this, we need to develop a system like the one I've described to
coordinate the work of the numerous spacecraft operators, but it's also essential that this system Q40
is one that establishes *trust* in the people that use it, both nationally and at a global level.

One interesting development …

TEST 4

PART 1

JULIE: Hello?
GREG: Oh, hello. Is that Julie Davison?
JULIE: Yes.
GREG: This is Greg Preston from the Employment Agency. We met last week when you came in to enquire about office work.
JULIE: Oh, that's right.
GREG: Now we've just had some details come in of a job which might interest you.
JULIE: OK.
GREG: So this is a position for a receptionist – I believe you've done that sort of work before? *Q1*
JULIE: Yes, I have, I worked in a sports centre for a couple of years before I got married and had the children.
GREG: Right. Well, this job's in Fordham, so not too far away for you, and it's at the medical centre there. *Q2*
JULIE: OK. So where exactly is that?
GREG: It's quite near the station, on Chastons Road. *Q3*
JULIE: Sorry?
GREG: Chastons Road – that's C-H-A–S-T-O-N-S.
JULIE: OK, thanks. So what would the work involve? Dealing with enquiries from patients?
GREG: Yes, and you'd also be involved in making appointments, whether face to face or on the phone. And rescheduling them if necessary. *Q4*
JULIE: Fine, that shouldn't be a problem.
GREG: And another of your duties would be keeping the centre's database up-to-date. Then you might have other general administrative duties as well, but those would be the main ones. *Q5*
JULIE: OK.
GREG: Now when the details came in, I immediately thought of you because one thing they do require is someone with experience, and you did mention your work at the sports centre when you came in to see us. *Q6*
JULIE: Yes, in fact I enjoyed that job. Is there anything else they're looking for?
GREG: Well, they say it's quite a high-pressure environment, they're always very busy, and patients are often under stress, so they want someone who can cope with that and stay calm, and at the same time be confident when interacting with the public. *Q7*
JULIE: Well, after dealing with three children all under five, I reckon I can cope with that.
GREG: I'm sure you can.
GREG: And then another thing they mention is that they're looking for someone with good IT skills …
JULIE: Not a problem.
GREG: So you'd be interested in following this up?
JULIE: Sure. When would it start?
GREG: Well, they're looking for someone from the beginning of next month, but I should tell you that this isn't a permanent job, it's temporary, so the contract would be just to the end of September. But they do say that there could be further opportunities after that. *Q8*
JULIE: OK. And what would the hours be?

GREG: Well, they want someone who can start at a quarter to eight in the morning – could you manage that?

JULIE: Yes, my husband would have to get the kids up and off to my mother's – she's going to be looking after them while I'm at work. What time would I finish?

GREG: One fifteen. Q9

JULIE: That should work out all right. I can pick the kids up on my way home, and then I'll have the afternoon with them. Oh, one thing … is there parking available for Q10
staff at the centre?

GREG: Yes, there is, and it's also on a bus route.

JULIE: Right. Well, I expect I'll have the car but it's good to know that.
OK, so where do I go from here?

GREG: Well, if you're happy for me to do so, I'll forward your CV and references, and then the best thing would probably be for you to phone them so they can arrange for an interview.

JULIE: Great. Well thank you very much.

GREG: You're welcome. Bye now.

JULIE: Bye.

PART 2

Good morning everyone, and welcome to the Museum of Farming Life. I understand it's your first visit here, so I'd like to give you some background information about the museum and then explain a little about what you can see during your visit.

So, where we're standing at the moment is the entrance to a large building that was
constructed in 1880 as the home of a local businessman, Alfred Palmer, of the Palmer biscuit Q11
factory. It was later sold and became a hall of residence for students in 1911, and a museum in 1951. In 2005, a modern extension was built to accommodate the museum's collections.

The museum's owned by the university, and apart from two rooms that are our offices, the
university uses the main part of the building. You may see students going into the building Q12
for lessons, but it's not open to museum visitors, I'm afraid. It's a shame because the interior architectural features are outstanding, especially the room that used to be the library.

Luckily, we've managed to keep entry to the museum free. This includes access to all the galleries, outdoor areas and the rooms for special exhibitions. We run activities for children
and students, such as the museum club, for which there's no charge. We do have a donation Q13
box just over there so feel free to give whatever amount you consider appropriate.

We do have a cloakroom, if you'd like to leave your coats and bags somewhere. Unlike other Q14
museums, photography is allowed here, so you might like to keep your cameras with you. You might be more comfortable not carrying around heavy rucksacks, though keep your coats and jackets on as it's quite cold in the museum garden today.

I'd like to tell you about the different areas of the museum.

Just inside, and outside the main gallery, we have an area called Four Seasons. Here you
can watch a four-minute animation of a woodland scene. It was designed especially for the Q15
museum by a group of young people on a film studies course, and it's beautiful. Children absolutely love it, but then, so do adults.

The main gallery's called Town and Country. It includes a photographic collection of prize-winning sheep and shepherds. Leaving Town and Country, you enter Farmhouse Kitchen, which is … well, self-explanatory. Here we have the oldest collection of equipment for making butter and cheese in the country. And this morning, a specialist cheesemaker will be giving demonstrations of how it's produced. You may even get to try some. Q16

After that, you can go in two directions. To the right is a staircase that takes you up to a landing from where you can look down on the galleries. To the left is a room called A Year on the Farm. There's lots of seating here as sometimes we use the room for school visits, so it's a good place to stop for a rest. If you're feeling competitive, you can take our memory test in which you answer questions about things you've seen in the museum. Q17

The next area's called Wagon Walk. This contains farm carts from nearly every part of the country. It's surprising how much regional variation there was. Beside the carts are display boards with information about each one. The carts are old and fragile, so we ask you to keep your children close to you and ensure they don't climb on the carts. Q18

From Wagon Walk, you can either make your way back to reception or go out into the garden – or even go back to take another look in the galleries. In the far corner of the garden is Bees are Magic, but we're redeveloping this area so you can't visit that at the moment. You can still buy our honey in the shop, though. Q19

Finally, there's The Pond, which contains all kinds of interesting wildlife. There are baby ducks that are only a few days old, as well as tiny frogs. The Pond isn't deep and there's a fence around it, so it's perfectly safe for children. Q20

PART 3

TUTOR: So now I want you to discuss the lesson we've just been watching on the video and think about the ways in which origami can be a useful educational tool. Can you all work with the person sitting next to you …

SEB: I had no idea that such a simple thing like folding squares of paper to make the shape of something like a bird could be such an amazing tool. It's made me see origami in a whole new light.

LIA: I know. It was interesting to see the educational skills the children were developing by doing origami. On the video you could see them really listening hard to make sure they did all the steps in the right order to make the bird. Q21/22

SEB: That's right. In this lesson they were working individually but it would also be interesting to see if the children could work out how to make something simple without being given any direction. That would help with building teamwork as well.

LIA: Yes, but much more of a challenge. One thing that really stood out for me was that the children were all having fun while being taught something new. Q21/22

SEB: Which is a key aim of any lesson with this age group. And although these kids had no problems with folding the paper, with younger children you could do origami to help practise fine motor skills.

LIA: Absolutely. Shall we talk about the individual children we saw on the video? I wrote all their names down and took some notes.

SEB: Yes, I did too.

LIA: OK, good. Let's start with Sid.

SEB: He was interesting because before they started doing the origami, he was being quite disruptive.

LIA: Yes. He really benefited from having to use his hands – it helped him to settle down and start concentrating. Q23

SEB: Yes, I noticed that too. What about Jack? I noticed he seemed to want to work things out for himself.

LIA: Mmm. You could see him trying out different things rather than asking the teacher for help. What did you make of Naomi? *Q24*

SEB: She seemed to be losing interest at one point but then she decided she wanted her mouse to be the best and that motivated her to try harder. *Q25*

LIA: She didn't seem satisfied with hers in the end, though.

SEB: No.

LIA: Anya was such a star. She listened so carefully and then produced the perfect bird with very little effort. *Q26*

SEB: Mmm – I think the teacher could have increased the level of difficulty for her.

LIA: Maybe. I think it was the first time Zara had come across origami.

SEB: She looked as if she didn't really get what was going on.

LIA: She seemed unsure about what she was supposed to do, but in the end hers didn't turn out too badly. *Q27*

SEB: Yeah. I'm sure it was a positive learning experience for her.

LIA: Mmm.

LIA: I think one reason why the origami activity worked so well in this class was that the teacher was well prepared.

SEB: Right. I think it would have taken me ages to prepare examples, showing each of the steps involved in making the bird. But that was a really good idea. The children could see what they were aiming for – and much better for them to be able to hold something, rather than just looking at pictures. *Q28*

LIA: Mmm – those physical examples supported her verbal explanations really well.

SEB: It's strange that origami isn't used more widely. Why do you think that is?

LIA: Well, teachers may just feel it's not that appealing to children who are used to doing everything on computers, especially boys. Even if they're aware of the benefits.

SEB: Oh, I don't know. It's no different to any other craft activity. I bet it's because so many teachers are clumsy like me. *Q29*

LIA: That's true – too much effort required if you're not good with your hands.

SEB: Well, anyway, I think we should try it out in our maths teaching practice with Year 3. I can see using origami is a really engaging way of reinforcing children's knowledge of geometric shapes, like they were doing in the video, but I think it would also work really well for presenting fractions, which is coming up soon. *Q30*

LIA: Good idea – that's something most of the kids in that class might struggle with. Origami would also be good practice for using symmetry – but I think they did that last term.

SEB: OK – well let's try and get some ideas together and plan the lesson next week.

TUTOR: OK, if you could all stop …

PART 4

The person I've chosen to talk about is the French writer Victor Hugo – many people have heard of him because his novel, *Les Misérables*, which he wrote in 1862, is famous around the world. It became a stage musical in the 1980s, and a film version was also released in 2012. So, some of us, I'm sure, have a pretty general idea of the plot, but we know much less about the author. Today, I'm going to provide a little more insight into this talented man and I'm going to talk particularly about the home he had on the island of Guernsey in the British Channel Islands. *Q31*

But first, his early career … as I've said, he was a writer, he was at the height of his career in Paris and he was very highly regarded by his colleagues. As far as literature was concerned, he was the leading figure of the Romantic movement. However, as well as being a literary genius, he also gave many speeches about issues like the level of poverty in his society. He *Q32* felt very strongly about this and about other areas where change was needed, like education. This kind of outspoken criticism was not well liked by the rulers of France and, eventually, the emperor – Napoleon III – told Victor Hugo to leave Paris and not return; in other words, he sent him into exile.

So Victor Hugo was forced to reside in other parts of Europe. Guernsey was actually his third *Q33* place of exile and he landed there in 1855. He produced a lot while on Guernsey – including *Les Misérables* – and to do this, he had to spend a great deal of time in the home that he had there. This was a property that he bought using the money he'd made in France from the *Q34* publication of a collection of his poetry. It was the only property he ever owned, and he was very proud of it.

The property Victor Hugo bought on Guernsey was a large, five-storey house in the capital town of St Peter Port and he lived there for 15 years, returning to France in 1870 when Napoleon's Empire collapsed. He decorated and furnished each level, or floor, of the house in unique and wonderful ways, and many people consider the inside of the house to be a 'work of art'. Today it's a museum that attracts 200,000 visitors a year.

He lived in the house with his family … and portraits of its members still hang in rooms on the *Q35* ground floor, along with drawings that he did during his travels that he felt were important to him. In other ground-floor rooms, there are huge tapestries that he would have designed and loved. The walls are covered in dark wood panelling that Victor Hugo created himself using *Q36* wooden furniture that he bought in the market. The items were relatively inexpensive, and he used them to create intricate carvings. They gave an atmosphere on the lower level that was shadowy and rather solemn.

On the next level of the house there are two impressive lounges, where he entertained his guests. One lounge has entirely red furnishings, such as sofas and wall coverings, and the other blue. There's a strong Chinese influence in these areas in things like the wallpaper *Q37* pattern and the lamps – which he would have made himself by copying original versions.

His library, where he left many of his favourite books, forms the hallway to the third floor and was a comfortable area where he could relax and enjoy his afternoons. And then, at the very top of the house, there's a room called the Lookout – called that because it looks out over the *Q38* harbour. In contrast to the rather dark lower levels, it's full of light and was like a glass office where he would write until lunchtime – often at his desk.

So, Victor Hugo was a man of many talents, but he was also true to his values. While living in his house on Guernsey, he entertained many other famous writers, but he also invited a large *Q39* group of local children from the deprived areas of the island to dinner once a week. What's more, he served them their food, which was an extraordinary gesture for the time period.

In 1927, the house was owned by his relatives, and they decided to donate it to the city of *Q40* Paris. It has since been restored using photographs from the period and, as I mentioned earlier, is now a museum that is open to the public.

Listening and Reading answer keys

TEST 1

LISTENING

Answer key with extra explanations in Resource Bank

Part 1, Questions 1–10

1 DW30 7YZ
2 24(th) April
3 dentist
4 parking
5 Claxby
6 late
7 evening
8 supermarket
9 pollution
10 storage

Part 2, Questions 11–20

11 C
12 A
13 A
14&15 *IN EITHER ORDER*
B
E
16 B
17 G
18 D
19 A
20 F

Part 3, Questions 21–30

21 A
22 B
23 A
24 C
25 B
26 A
27&28 *IN EITHER ORDER*
B
E
29&30 *IN EITHER ORDER*
A
C

Part 4, Questions 31–40

31 fences
32 family
33 helicopters
34 stress
35 sides
36 breathing
37 feet
38 employment
39 weapons
40 tourism

If you score …

0–19	20–28	29–40
you are unlikely to get an acceptable score under examination conditions and we recommend that you spend a lot of time improving your English before you take IELTS.	you may get an acceptable score under examination conditions but we recommend that you think about having more practice or lessons before you take IELTS.	you are likely to get an acceptable score under examination conditions but remember that different institutions will find different scores acceptable.

TEST 1

READING

Answer key with extra explanations in Resource Bank

Reading Section 1, Questions 1–14

1 TRUE
2 FALSE
3 FALSE
4 TRUE
5 FALSE
6 NOT GIVEN
7 TRUE
8 A
9 F
10 B
11 C
12 F
13 E
14 B

Reading Section 2, Questions 15–27

15 (CE) mark
16 tests
17 engineer
18 control measures
19 (lifting) crew
20 barriers
21 banksman
22 injuries
23 win
24 expectations
25 solution
26 policy
27 recommendation

Reading Section 3, Questions 28–40

28 vii
29 i
30 vi
31 iii
32 viii
33 ii
34 sticks
35 infertile
36 Poland
37 loyalty
38 D
39 C
40 A

If you score …

0–26	27–32	33–40
you are unlikely to get an acceptable score under examination conditions and we recommend that you spend a lot of time improving your English before you take IELTS.	you may get an acceptable score under examination conditions but we recommend that you think about having more practice or lessons before you take IELTS.	you are likely to get an acceptable score under examination conditions but remember that different institutions will find different scores acceptable.

TEST 2

LISTENING

Answer key with extra explanations in Resource Bank

Part 1, Questions 1–10

1 training
2 discount
3 taxi
4 service
5 English
6 Wivenhoe
7 equipment
8 9.75
9 deliveries
10 Sunday

Part 2, Questions 11–20

11&12 *IN EITHER ORDER*
B
E
13&14 *IN EITHER ORDER*
B
C
15 G
16 C
17 D
18 B
19 H
20 A

Part 3, Questions 21–30

21 C
22 A
23 B
24 B
25&26 *IN EITHER ORDER*
A
B
27 D
28 A
29 C
30 F

Part 4, Questions 31–40

31 convenient
32 suits
33 tailor
34 profession
35 visible
36 string(s)
37 waist(s)
38 perfume
39 image
40 handbag

If you score …

0–18	19–28	29–40
you are unlikely to get an acceptable score under examination conditions and we recommend that you spend a lot of time improving your English before you take IELTS.	you may get an acceptable score under examination conditions but we recommend that you think about having more practice or lessons before you take IELTS.	you are likely to get an acceptable score under examination conditions but remember that different institutions will find different scores acceptable.

TEST 2

READING

Answer key with extra explanations in Resource Bank

Reading Section 1, Questions 1–14

1 D
2 A
3 E
4 B
5 D
6 F
7 C
8 A
9 TRUE
10 FALSE
11 TRUE
12 NOT GIVEN
13 FALSE
14 NOT GIVEN

Reading Section 2, Questions 15–27

15 absenteeism
16 soda
17 fruit
18 fridge
19 bikes
20 showers
21 surveys
22 aprons
23 board
24 money
25 appliances
26 Labels
27 storeroom

Reading Section 3, Questions 28–40

28 E
29 C
30 A
31 E
32 D
33 A
34 C
35 C
36 fabric
37 instructions
38 geometric
39 newspaper
40 knitwear

If you score …

0–25	26–32	33–40
you are unlikely to get an acceptable score under examination conditions and we recommend that you spend a lot of time improving your English before you take IELTS.	you may get an acceptable score under examination conditions but we recommend that you think about having more practice or lessons before you take IELTS.	you are likely to get an acceptable score under examination conditions but remember that different institutions will find different scores acceptable.

TEST 3

LISTENING

Answer key with extra explanations in Resource Bank

Part 1, Questions 1–10

1 Marrowfield
2 relative
3 socialise / socialize
4 full
5 Domestic Life
6 clouds
7 timing
8 Animal Magic
9 (animal) movement
10 dark

Part 2, Questions 11–20

11&12 *IN EITHER ORDER*
B
C
13&14 *IN EITHER ORDER*
B
D
15 C
16 B
17 B
18 C
19 A
20 A

Part 3, Questions 21–30

21&22 *IN EITHER ORDER*
A
E
23&24 *IN EITHER ORDER*
B
D
25 G
26 E
27 B
28 C
29 F
30 A

Part 4, Questions 31–40

31 technical
32 cheap
33 thousands
34 identification
35 tracking
36 military
37 location
38 prediction
39 database
40 trust

If you score …

0–18	19–28	29–40
you are unlikely to get an acceptable score under examination conditions and we recommend that you spend a lot of time improving your English before you take IELTS.	you may get an acceptable score under examination conditions but we recommend that you think about having more practice or lessons before you take IELTS.	you are likely to get an acceptable score under examination conditions but remember that different institutions will find different scores acceptable.

TEST 3

READING

Answer key with extra explanations in Resource Bank

Reading Section 1, Questions 1–14

1 F
2 B
3 F
4 D
5 E
6 B
7 A
8 TRUE
9 NOT GIVEN
10 TRUE
11 FALSE
12 FALSE
13 TRUE
14 TRUE

Reading Section 2, Questions 15–27

15 sharing
16 mileage
17 night
18 replacement
19 cover
20 complaints
21 wires
22 chairs
23 mirrors
24 carpets
25 drawers
26 adjustable
27 holders

Reading Section 3, Questions 28–40

28 C
29 F
30 D
31 B
32 F
33 C
34 B
35 D
36 A
37 C
38 (fine) gravel
39 animals
40 (crushed) brick

If you score …

0–25	26–32	33–40
you are unlikely to get an acceptable score under examination conditions and we recommend that you spend a lot of time improving your English before you take IELTS.	you may get an acceptable score under examination conditions but we recommend that you think about having more practice or lessons before you take IELTS.	you are likely to get an acceptable score under examination conditions but remember that different institutions will find different scores acceptable.

TEST 4

LISTENING

Answer key with extra explanations in Resource Bank

Part 1, Questions 1–10

1 receptionist
2 Medical
3 Chastons
4 appointments
5 database
6 experience
7 confident
8 temporary
9 1.15
10 parking

Part 2, Questions 11–20

11 B
12 A
13 A
14 C
15 F
16 G
17 E
18 A
19 C
20 B

Part 3, Questions 21–30

21&22 *IN EITHER ORDER*
B
D
23 D
24 A
25 C
26 G
27 F
28 A
29 B
30 C

Part 4, Questions 31–40

31 plot
32 poverty
33 Europe
34 poetry
35 drawings
36 furniture
37 lamps
38 harbour / harbor
39 children
40 relatives

If you score ...

0–17	18–27	28–40
you are unlikely to get an acceptable score under examination conditions and we recommend that you spend a lot of time improving your English before you take IELTS.	you may get an acceptable score under examination conditions but we recommend that you think about having more practice or lessons before you take IELTS.	you are likely to get an acceptable score under examination conditions but remember that different institutions will find different scores acceptable.

TEST 4

READING

Answer key with extra explanations in Resource Bank

Reading Section 1, Questions 1–14

1 B
2 C
3 F
4 A
5 C
6 D
7 C
8 FALSE
9 FALSE
10 NOT GIVEN
11 TRUE
12 TRUE
13 NOT GIVEN
14 TRUE

Reading Section 2, Questions 15–27

15 oxygen
16 yearly
17 beard
18 solvents
19 rack
20 straps
21 sunlight
22 footwear
23 padding
24 handrails
25 trolleys
26 overreach
27 rotation

Reading Section 3, Questions 28–40

28 vi
29 i
30 vii
31 iv
32 iii
33 viii
34 v
35 fungi
36 horizon
37 surface
38 landscape
39 galaxies
40 gardens

If you score …

0–24	25–31	32–40
you are unlikely to get an acceptable score under examination conditions and we recommend that you spend a lot of time improving your English before you take IELTS.	you may get an acceptable score under examination conditions but we recommend that you think about having more practice or lessons before you take IELTS.	you are likely to get an acceptable score under examination conditions but remember that different institutions will find different scores acceptable.

Sample Writing answers

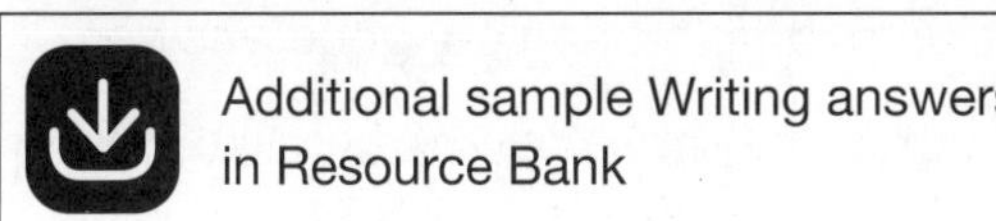

Additional sample Writing answers in Resource Bank

TEST 1, WRITING TASK 1

This model has been prepared by an examiner as an example of a very good answer.

Dear Mia

It's great to hear from you; your project sounds really interesting. I'd be happy to tell you about Tet in Vietnam.

Tet is short for Tết Nguyên Đán and it's our New Year according to the lunar calendar. It's the first day of spring and it's usually in January or February. It's really important to us as it's a chance for the family to come together and we visit the graves of our ancestors. It's probably the biggest festival in Vietnam and it's a public holiday. We say if good things happen on the first day of the new year, the whole year will be full of blessings.

I always loved it as a child because I would get a red envelope with money inside it from the older members of the family. Now I like visiting friends and the extended family on the week of Tet and enjoying the lovely candied fruits that we have on this occasion.

I hope that helps. Do ask if there's anything else you'd like to know.

All the best

Here are comments from another examiner:

> This is a full response to the task. The candidate addresses the first two bullet points in the second paragraph, then covers the last bullet in the third, but could add more about how New Year is celebrated. They mention [*the biggest festival … public holiday*] but give no details about how it is celebrated.
>
> However, the enthusiastic tone is just right for a letter to a friend, and progression in the response is clear. There are some effective linking expressions [*according to* | *because* | *Now*], although in the second paragraph, most sentences start with [*It's*], so a wider range would improve the response.
>
> The range of vocabulary includes some less common items and some good collocation [*come together* | *good things happen*], but it could be wider. Similarly, there is a mix of grammatical structures, including conditionals [*if*], but generally, the range is limited with simple structures and short, compound sentences. Overall, this is an appropriate and engaging response. To improve it, the range of cohesive devices and grammatical structures could be widened.

TEST 1, WRITING TASK 2

This model has been prepared by an examiner as an example of a very good answer.

Job seekers often question whether it is better to work for a large or a small company. I would personally prefer to work for a larger company, but I'd like to consider the advantages and disadvantages of both.

In general, larger companies can support their employees more effectively because they have access to more resources. These could include higher salaries, end-of-year bonuses, and other perks such as an excellent food service and even sports facilities. Large companies may also contribute more to your professional development, offering regular conferences and training courses.

The size of a large company is also an indication of their success, meaning that it can offer greater stability. There is also a better chance for promotion and career development in companies with many departments and a larger management structure. Of course, advancement may not come easily because it is hard to stand out when many employees are vying for the same role.

In small companies, you may feel less like a number and that your efforts actually make a difference. You will also need to wear different hats, which helps you develop a skill set that might not be possible in a larger company. The downside is a higher chance of strained relationships because working in close proximity with the same small group of people every day can be challenging. Small companies can also be unstable. If they lose a large account or consumer tastes change, your position could suddenly become precarious.

Based on the above, I'd say that the kind of company you work for depends on personal preference, but your future career prospects may be better in a large company.

Here are comments from another examiner:

> This response covers both aspects of the task, including the pros and cons of each type of workplace, with some useful detail and good supporting ideas. Ideas are logically organised and cohesion is very well managed throughout.
>
> There are a range of linkers [*Of course* | *Based on the above*] and other cohesive devices [*both* | *your* | *their* | *which*], which means it is easy to read. Paragraphing is generally good, with the introduction and conclusion sitting separately. However, the second and third paragraphs would be better combined, as they both address 'large' companies.
>
> Vocabulary is strong and there are some natural and sophisticated examples [*vying for* | *wear different hats* | *strained relationships*]. Grammar is flexible and accurate, with a range of structures including modals [*can* | *may* | *could*] and conditionals [*If*] as part of complex, multi-clause sentences. Errors are rare.
>
> This is a good example of a high-level response.

TEST 2, WRITING TASK 1

This model has been prepared by an examiner as an example of a very good answer.

Dear Sir or Madam,

I am excited to be starting work experience at the RRN Broadcasting Corporation on 10 June and I would like to thank you very much for this opportunity. I am grateful to have the chance to gain some insight into the industry I wish to work in one day.

As I mentioned in my interview, I am especially interested in community television and would love to build on my skills in sound engineering. Besides this, I am hoping to develop my soft skills in areas such as teamwork, problem solving and effective communication.

I was wondering if it has been decided which team I will be working with and whether I will have a mentor assigned to me. I would like to prepare ahead of time if possible by doing some research. I also wanted to clarify whether I will be at the studio in Newtown or the headquarters in the city centre.

I am looking forward to hearing from you.

Kind regards

Here are comments from another examiner:

> This is a strong response to the task; it addresses all three bullet points and uses a suitable tone to communicate with the manager of the organisation. The response is presented in the correct letter format, with an appropriate ending, and there is clear progression throughout the letter.
>
> The range of vocabulary is wide and precise [*gain some insight into* | *develop my soft skills* | *mentor assigned*], without errors. The writing contains a wide range of structures, including conditionals [*if*] and passives [*it has been decided*], with accurate multi-clause sentences.
>
> This is a good example of a higher-level response.

TEST 2, WRITING TASK 2

This model has been prepared by an examiner as an example of a very good answer.

Some people say that we form an opinion about a person within thirty seconds of meeting them. A person's clothing, facial expression, and even the way they shake hands can have a profound effect on our judgement. But is this natural human tendency good or bad?

There is something unfair about our inclination to judge people too quickly. Many people have had unfortunate life experiences that can affect their confidence when meeting new people. Shyness may make them appear aloof and cold, but this initially icy persona melts away when we allow them a bit of time to warm up. Others do not have the means to dress in a way that leaves an impression. Inevitably, if we write people off too quickly, we could miss out on potential friendships, business opportunities and even romantic relationships.

There is another side to this that is also worth considering. We are all aware of the effect first impressions can have. There is even a saying: you don't get a second chance to make a first impression. Awareness of this reality should motivate us to always treat people in a friendly, respectful manner. If we strive to make a good impression on the people we meet, it increases our overall happiness and sense of well-being.

On balance, there is no doubt that judging people too quickly can have negative consequences. But knowing the power of first impressions can keep us on our toes, motivating us to question how we come across to others. Aside from this, the ability to read people quickly could also prevent us from being easily taken in by somebody with ulterior motives.

Here are comments from another examiner:

This response presents both sides of the argument and the ending concludes that forming impressions early can be either positive or negative. The second paragraph presents the downsides of judging too rapidly: the impact of low confidence, being shy or not having smart clothes. It also notes that people could miss out on friendships, opportunities and romance if they judge too harshly.

The third paragraph is not entirely relevant. The question asks about the evaluation people make about the 'kind of person' and whether 'we like them' but this paragraph mainly gives advice on how to behave when meeting new people. It should be more aligned to the question and present the advantages of forming early impressions.

There is a very wide range of vocabulary with some higher-level items [*affect their confidence* | *aloof* | *icy persona* | *strive to make* | *come across*]. Overall, the response includes a variety of accurate complex grammatical structures, with many long sentences containing a number of clauses.

Vocabulary and grammatical structures are very strong, accurate and flexible throughout. To improve the response, the third paragraph could present more clearly the advantages of quick decisions about the people we meet.

TEST 3, WRITING TASK 1

This model has been prepared by an examiner as an example of a very good answer.

Dear Sir or Madam

I am writing to complain about the information on your website and the service I received at Central Station. Yesterday my elderly uncle and I arrived at Central intending to use the tickets we had purchased online to travel to Newcastle at 5.50pm. Unfortunately, we were told that our tickets were for off-peak and we couldn't use them.

When I bought the tickets, it was not clear on the website that they were just for certain times. This needs to be clarified on your website as I can't be the only one who has made this mistake. However, what really upset me was the unhelpful manner of the staff. When we asked what to do, instead of helping us to pay the difference and catch our train, the attendant waved us in the direction of a ticket machine with a long queue. We missed our train and waited an hour for the next one. Please train your personnel to be more proactive in future.

I hope you find this feedback useful and take it on board.

Yours faithfully

Here are comments from another examiner:

> This is a very strong response to the task: all three bullet points are addressed with a good level of detail, and the tone is suitable for a letter of complaint. There is clear progression throughout the letter and a very natural style.
>
> The range of vocabulary is wide and includes many higher-level items [*unhelpful manner of* | *pay the difference* | *direction of* | *proactive*]. There is only one slip [*off-peak* / off-peak travel].
>
> Overall, the response includes a variety of complex grammatical structures [*intending to use*], with numerous long sentences containing a number of clauses, including past perfect and modal forms [*had purchased* | *couldn't use*].
>
> This is already a very high-level response. To improve it, the final bullet point could be developed further, perhaps with an example of how the staff could be 'more proactive'.

TEST 3, WRITING TASK 2

This model has been prepared by an examiner as an example of a very good answer.

It is increasingly common for people to hold down more than one job. Gone are the days when people could rely on one source of income to satisfy all their financial needs. I would like to consider the reasons for this change and outline its advantages and disadvantages.

People take on extra work because making ends meet has become so challenging. In recent years the cost of living has risen exponentially, making it a real challenge to break even at the end of the month. Additionally, advertising companies relentlessly promote the idea that more wealth means more happiness, a concept that many people believe. They may take on freelance jobs or weekend work in the hope of improving their lot in life.

A person with more than one job may experience several benefits. Diversifying your skills and gaining more experience can make you more employable when negotiating the highly competitive job market. Avoiding putting all your eggs in one basket is also a wise move as you have something to fall back on if one source of income stops.

There are also many downsides to this situation. Working for more than one company can quickly leave a person feeling overworked and burnt out. It also leaves limited time for being with family and friends or doing things you enjoy. What's more, when you are spread too thin, you may produce poor-quality work.

Overall, I think it is important to remain balanced. Having an additional source of income can be beneficial if you keep work in its place, but it is not worth damaging your health and relationships for the sake of a slightly larger bank balance.

Here are comments from another examiner:

> This is a strong response. The candidate has addressed both questions and provided a range of extended ideas.
>
> The reasons given for having more than one job include the need to earn more to keep up with the [*cost of living*] and the idea, sold to people by advertising, that we should earn as much as possible [*more wealth means more happiness*].
>
> The pros and cons of having more than one job are well covered. Advantages include increasing your skills and experience to make you more employable and avoiding putting [*all your eggs in one basket*] in case you lose one job. Disadvantages include feeling [*overworked*] or [*burnt out*], and [*limited time*] to spend with family and friends and on hobbies, and producing [*poor-quality work*].

The response is logically organised with well-managed cohesion. There are some very good linkers [*Gone are the days when* | *Additionally* | *What's more*] and accurate reference and substitution.

Vocabulary is accurate and wide ranging [*satisfy … financial needs* | *take on* | *risen exponentially* | *break even* | *improving their lot*] with some sophisticated resource [*putting all your eggs in one basket* | *burnt out* | *spread too thin*]. Similarly, the range of grammatical structures is wide and flexible.

This is a very good example of a higher-level response.

TEST 4, WRITING TASK 1

This model has been prepared by an examiner as an example of a very good answer.

Dear Ms Karim,

Thank you very much again for sending me on the Workplace Safety course. It was valuable training and I now feel a lot more confident that I know how to prevent accidents in the factory. We covered points such as safe storage, keeping access ways clear and fire safety.

I can report that I have already used the skills I learned; when I noticed some cables that were a trip hazard and also a large bin that was partially blocking the exit, I was able to identify and fix those problems straight away.

I understand that employees who started working with us this year have already received this training as part of their orientation but for those who have been here longer, it would be a good opportunity to refresh and add to their knowledge.

It is a well-run course that is very relevant to our workplace and I am grateful for the opportunity.

Many thanks

Here are comments from another examiner:

> This is a good response to the task: it addresses all three bullet points, uses a suitable tone to communicate with an employer and is presented in the correct letter format. There is clear progression throughout the letter, but there could be more evidence to justify why the course might not be suitable for colleagues (the final bullet point). There are some effective cohesive devices [*that* | *those who*], but a wider range of linking expressions than [*and* | *but*] would improve the final rating.
>
> Vocabulary is used well, and there is some effective collocation [*prevent accidents* | *trip hazard* | *partially blocking*]. Grammatical structures include simple and complex examples [*started working with us* | *have been here longer*], but most of the letter is in the past simple and past simple tenses.
>
> To achieve the highest scores, the candidate would need to include a wider range of cohesive devices and grammatical structures. They could improve the response by providing further suggestions on why the course may not be suitable for other colleagues. Overall, it is a good response.

TEST 4, WRITING TASK 2

This model has been prepared by an examiner as an example of a very good answer.

It is true that nothing in life is permanent except change. Changes in society and our own lives are inevitable. We all get older, friends and family move away, and our employment situation can suddenly change. Understandably, many people wish everything could stay the same. In this essay, I would like to consider the reasons for this view and explain why it is better to embrace change.

Wanting to feel in control of our lives is perfectly normal. We often feel vulnerable when events in society occur which are beyond our control or when we cannot be sure of the outcome of something. The uncertainty caused by the COVID-19 pandemic is an example of this. Changes in our personal circumstances can also be hard to accept. For example, when a friend or family member moves away, we may experience a deep sense of loss. Ironically, even good changes can bring uncertainty. If we receive a promotion, we may struggle with imposter syndrome and wrestle with a fear of failure.

Despite these perfectly natural feelings, I think it is good to embrace change. Since change is unavoidable, it is much better to accept reality than to become consumed by negative thinking. When we remain positive, we may find that a change actually benefits us in the long run. Adapting to change also helps us develop resilience, a quality that can help us face an obstacle and see an opportunity in it.

As highlighted above, sooner or later, we will all face change. While change is unsettling, it is vital to keep focused on the positive aspects of our circumstances. Doing so can help us unlock new opportunities we didn't know were available to us.

Here are comments from another examiner:

> This letter is a high-level response that covers all aspects of the question. In the second paragraph, reasons are presented on why people in society as a whole and individuals might resist change. Then, the third paragraph gives clear reasons to suggest that, overall, this is a positive process. The position is consistent and the conclusion ties both areas together for a strong finish.
>
> Ideas are logically organised. Cohesive devices [*Ironically* | *Despite these* | *As highlighted above* | *Doing so can*] are used highly effectively and paragraphing is helpful.
>
> Vocabulary is natural and sophisticated [*embrace change* | *deep sense of loss* | *consumed by negative thinking* | *develop resilience*]. Sentence structure demonstrates full flexibility, with a wide range of complex examples within a range of largely error-free multi-clause sentences.
>
> Little needs to be added to improve the rating other than possibly an example to illustrate why changes should be seen as positive, in the third paragraph. However, this is a very good high-level response.

Sample answer sheets

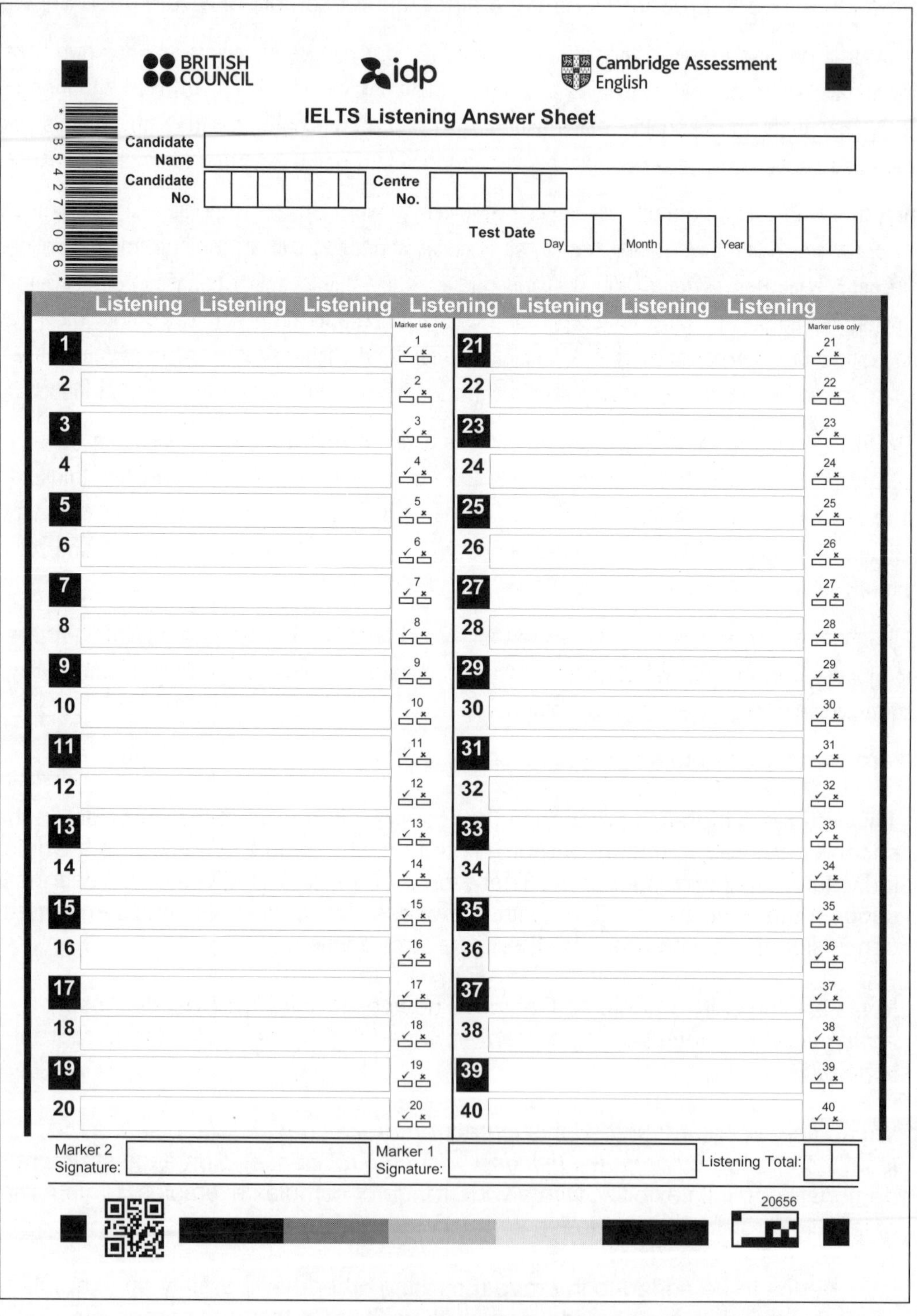

BRITISH COUNCIL idp Cambridge Assessment English

IELTS Reading Answer Sheet

Candidate Name

Candidate No. | Centre No.

Test Module ☐ Academic ☐ General Training | Test Date Day Month Year

Reading Reading Reading Reading Reading Reading Reading

No.	Answer	Marker use only	No.	Answer	Marker use only
1		1 ✓ ✗	21		21 ✓ ✗
2		2 ✓ ✗	22		22 ✓ ✗
3		3 ✓ ✗	23		23 ✓ ✗
4		4 ✓ ✗	24		24 ✓ ✗
5		5 ✓ ✗	25		25 ✓ ✗
6		6 ✓ ✗	26		26 ✓ ✗
7		7 ✓ ✗	27		27 ✓ ✗
8		8 ✓ ✗	28		28 ✓ ✗
9		9 ✓ ✗	29		29 ✓ ✗
10		10 ✓ ✗	30		30 ✓ ✗
11		11 ✓ ✗	31		31 ✓ ✗
12		12 ✓ ✗	32		32 ✓ ✗
13		13 ✓ ✗	33		33 ✓ ✗
14		14 ✓ ✗	34		34 ✓ ✗
15		15 ✓ ✗	35		35 ✓ ✗
16		16 ✓ ✗	36		36 ✓ ✗
17		17 ✓ ✗	37		37 ✓ ✗
18		18 ✓ ✗	38		38 ✓ ✗
19		19 ✓ ✗	39		39 ✓ ✗
20		20 ✓ ✗	40		40 ✓ ✗

Marker 2 Signature: | Marker 1 Signature: | Reading Total:

61788

BRITISH COUNCIL idp Cambridge Assessment English

2154789321

IELTS Writing Answer Sheet - TASK 1

Candidate Name

Candidate No. **Centre No.**

Test Module ☐ Academic ☐ General Training **Test Date** Day Month Year

If you need more space to write your answer, use an additional sheet and write in the space provided to indicate how many sheets you are using: Sheet of

Writing Task 1 Writing Task 1 Writing Task 1 Writing Task 1

Do not write below this line

Do not write in this area. Please continue your answer on the other side of this sheet.

23505

BRITISH COUNCIL idp Cambridge Assessment English

7834418290

IELTS Writing Answer Sheet - TASK 2

Candidate Name

Candidate No. **Centre No.**

Test Module ☐ Academic ☐ General Training **Test Date** Day Month Year

If you need more space to write your answer, use an additional sheet and write in the space provided to indicate how many sheets you are using: Sheet ☐ of ☐

Writing Task 2 Writing Task 2 Writing Task 2 Writing Task 2

Do not write below this line

Do not write in this area. Please continue your answer on the other side of this sheet.

39507

Acknowledgements

The authors and publishers acknowledge the following sources of copyright material and are grateful for the permissions granted. While every effort has been made, it has not always been possible to identify the sources of all the material used, or to trace all copyright holders. If any omissions are brought to our notice, we will be happy to include the appropriate acknowledgements on reprinting and in the next update to the digital edition, as applicable.

Key: L = Listening; R = Reading

Text

L1: Sue Watt and *Travel Africa* Magazine for the text adapted from 'How to translocate an elephant' by Sue Watt. Copyright © 2022 *Travel Africa* Magazine. Published by Gecko Publishing Ltd. Reproduced with permission; **R1:** Citizens Advice for the text adapted from 'If your clothes have been lost or damaged by a dry cleaner' by Citizens Advice, available at https://www.citizensadvice.org.uk/consumer/somethings-gone-wrong-with-a-purchase/dry-cleaner/ as of 28.11.2022, 13:00 GMT. Copyright © 2022 Citizens Advice. Reproduced with permission; The Reading Agency for the text adapted from 'Reading groups for everyone-teenvision'. Copyright © The Reading Agency 2022. Reproduced with kind permission; Safe Workers owned and operated by Blue Indian Media Ltd for the text adapted from 'Mechanical lifting equipment – shifting heavy loads safely' by Norman Thomson, 06.01.2022. Copyright 2022 © Safe Workers. Reproduced with kind permission; *Training* magazine for the text adapted from 'How to handle customer complaints' by Lorri Freifeld, 18.06.2013. Copyright © 2013 Lakewood Media Group LLC. Reproduced with kind permission; *The Guardian* for the text adapted from 'Storks are back in Britain – and they're a beacon of hope for all of us' by Isabella Tree, *The Guardian*, 08.07.2019. Copyright © 2019 Guardian News & Media Limited. Reproduced with permission; **R2:** *The Independent* for the text adapted from '10 best sleeping bags for camping, festivals and trekking adventures' by Tamara Hinson, *The Independent*, 31.08.2022. Copyright © 2022 Independent Digital News and Media Limited. Reproduced with permission; Spread the Word for the text adapted from 'Life-Writing-Prize-2019-Rules'. Copyright © Spread the Word. Reproduced with permission; 6Q for the text adapted from '57 great ways to encourage better employee health' by Miles Burke. Copyright © 2022 6Q. Reproduced with kind permission; *The Telegraph* for the text adapted from 'A home-sewing revival: the return of Clothkits' by Clover Stroud, *The Telegraph*,10.06.2010. Copyright © Telegraph Media Group Limited 2010. Reproduced with permission; **R3:** *Safety+Health* magazine, National Safety Council for the text adapted from 'Recognizing hidden dangers: 25 steps to a safer office' by Lauretta Claussen, 01.06.2011. Copyright © 2011 National Safety Council. Reproduced with kind permission; World History Encyclopedia by World History Publishing for the text adapted from 'Roman Roads' by Mark Cartwright, 17.09.2014, available at https://www.worldhistory.org/article/758/roman-roads/#ci_author_and_copyright. Copyright © World History Publishing. Reproduced with permission; **R4:** *The Independent* for the text adapted from '7 best ice cream makers for frozen treats at home this summer' by Katie Gregory, *The Independent*, 02.08.2022. Copyright © 2022 Independent Digital News & Media Ltd. Reproduced with permission; Mullion Cove Hotel for the text adapted on photography course led by Carla Regler. Copyright © 2017 Mullion Cove Hotel. Reproduced with kind permission; WorkSafe for the text adapted from 'Respiratory protective equipment – advice for workers', November 2016. Copyright © 2016 WorkSafe. Reproduced with kind permission; Syon Geographical for the text adapted from 'Night photography from dusk till dawn' by Michael Black, December 2017. Copyright © Syon Geographical. Reproduced with permission.

Audio

Audio production by dsound recording Ltd.

Typesetting

Typeset by QBS Learning.

URLs